THE GOSPEL IN TEN WORDS

PAUL ELLIS

KINGSPRESS
Birkenhead, New Zealand

The Gospel in Ten Words

ISBN: 978-1-927230-00-8
Copyright © 2012 by Paul Ellis

Published by KingsPress
This title is also available as an ebook. Visit www.KingsPress.org for information.

Dedication: This is for everyone.

ENDORSEMENTS

"Ever felt afraid that the grace of God sounds too good to be true? I have known Paul for about 20 years. He is a man of immense integrity and humility. When he writes something he means it! Many are looking for truth they can rely on. In *The Gospel in Ten Words*, Paul delivers this big time. Read and be in awe of how good God is!"

— ROB RUFUS
senior pastor, City Church International, Hong Kong

"Paul Ellis has written the definitive book on the gospel! His *Gospel in Ten Words* will go down as one of the best books I have ever read on the subject. After I finished reading it, I immediately reread it again, it was just that good! This is a book, you will read, reread and go back to reference it again and again. It is a book you will want to share with all your friends and total strangers as well. I would recommend buying a case of them."

— ED ELLIOTT, aka The Vagabond Evangelist
President, World of Life Outreach

"Dr. Paul Ellis's book, *The Gospel in Ten Words*, is liberating! It simplifies the gospel of Jesus Christ, and reveals its life transforming power."

— PETER M. KAIRUZ
CEO of CBN Asia and Host of *The 700 Club Asia*

"If your walk with God has become a laboring crawl, then Paul's book, *The Gospel in Ten Words*, is exactly what you need. Each chapter is an exhilarating view of the gospel of Jesus—I'm not kidding—and the reader is amazed at what is found. In the same way a weary and struggling hiker is dazzled by a sudden meadow opening before him, we find that the struggle is over and all that is left is to marvel and breathe. That's the unending view Paul Ellis offers—the stunning good news God intends for us all. This is the book I'd choose for anyone considering a journey with God, whether it's the beginning or a going on."

— RALPH HARRIS
author of *God's Astounding Opinion of You*

"One of the best books I have ever read. The light of the glorious gospel of Christ flooded my heart as I read this book. This book is all about Jesus Christ and his finished work on the cross. I now have a clearer understanding on who I am and what I have because of what Jesus Christ has done."

> — JUN YU
> senior pastor Jesus Faith Christian Fellowship, the Philippines

"This book is simply captivating! It's like looking at the gospel of grace in a 360° panoramic shot. Written with amazing clarity and practicality, *The Gospel in Ten Words* oozes good news on every page."

> — CORNEL MARAIS
> author of *So You Think Your Mind is Renewed?*

"I love *The Gospel in Ten Words*. This is revelation that will come as a wonderful surprise for the new believer, as well as for many who have thought they understood the gospel but have been bound in tradition-based thinking. With grace and joyful power, Paul systematically replaces misconceptions with the bedrock realities of the good news that God has given to all people. I will be recommending this book to everybody!"

> — JACK STRADWICK
> senior pastor, Fusion Church, New Zealand

"Paul Ellis is one of only a handful of people that I'm aware of who can present the gospel of grace in a way that is not only easy to understand, but also empowers those who believe to embrace the supernatural power of God. Read this book, whether you think you understand the gospel or not. It will change you."

> — RYAN RHOADES
> founder of RevivalOrRiots.org

"I have been reading Paul's writings for a few years now and I have often been encouraged and strengthened by his revelation on the gospel. *The Gospel in Ten Words* will strengthen you in the too good to be true news of a God that loves us more than we know and who has given us more than we use. This book will help you unlock God's love and full provision in Christ."

> — WAYNE DUNCAN
> senior pastor, Coastlands Christian Church, South Africa

Contents

OUT OF THE JUNGLE

When World War II came to an end, it was a time of great joy and celebration. Proverbial swords were beaten into plowshares, prisoners were set free, and millions of soldiers went home to their families. But one man, Second Lieutenant Hiroo Onoda of the Imperial Japanese Army, chose not to believe broadcasts announcing the end of the war. For the next 29 years Lieutenant Onoda hid in the jungles of the Philippines refusing to come home.

Knowing he was still out there, the authorities tried to reach him with the news. However, Onoda dismissed leaflets left by the islanders as enemy propaganda. He considered letters, family photos, and newspapers dropped from planes as nothing more than clever tricks.

In 1974 a Japanese college student made it his personal quest to track down the holdout. After trekking through the jungle the student found the old soldier and befriended him, but he could not convince him to surrender.

Eventually, the Japanese Government sent Onoda's former commanding officer into the jungle with orders for him to stand down. Relieved of duty, Onoda emptied the bullets from his rifle and turned in his weapon. For him the war was finally over. He returned home to a hero's welcome.[1]

For three decades Lieutenant Onoda was engaged in a war that existed only in his mind against an imaginary enemy he both feared and distrusted. This is how some people relate to God. They're opposed to God in their minds or they think God is gunning for them on account of their sin. They have not heard there has been a cessation of hostilities, that the war has been won and the Prince of Peace now sits on the throne. Ignorant of this good news and fearful of God they are lying low in the jungles of religion or godless self-deception. God hates them — or so they think. His anger is mounting. They are not sure what God is doing now but they expect him to show up one day, and when he does there will be hell to pay.

Why I wrote this book

I wrote this book for one simple reason: most people haven't heard the gospel. How do I know? Because most are unsure of who God is and what he thinks of them. Or perhaps they have heard the good news but they don't believe it; it doesn't fit in their grid. So they live under a lie, refusing to come home.

Sadly this is just as true of Christians as unbelievers.

In ten years as a pastor and forty years as a churchgoer I have met thousands of believers around the world. Every single one of them would tell you they believe the gospel. But the fruit of their lives often reveals a different story. Instead of reaping from the gospel of peace, they are plowing the hard ground of D.I.Y. religion. Instead of drawing with joy from the wells of salvation, they are baking bricks in the pits of performance-based churchianity.

Why am I convinced that most people don't know the gospel? Because they have no joy. Their mouths aren't filled with laughter and their tongues don't sing of the great things God has done for them. To paraphrase Shakespeare, the joy's the thing:

> But the angel said to them, "Do not be afraid. I bring you good news of great joy that will be for all the people." (Luke 2:10)

The angel said the gospel would bring great joy to all people. Those who receive the gospel ought to be the happiest, most joyful people in the world. Yet many believers are far from joyful. They may be smiling on the outside, but on the inside they are anxious, insecure, and battling with guilt and condemnation. Fearful of upsetting a touchy God they are trying to do the right thing and make themselves pleasing to the Lord. But since they are never sure if they have done enough they have no peace. Others are running hard after the favor of God but they never seem to arrive. They study the scriptures, fast and pray, and do all they are told to do, but the promised blessings of the Christian life—God's forgiveness, acceptance, provision and so on—always seem just out of reach. They're sweating on the hamster wheel of Christian service and going nowhere fast.

Squeezed between the demands of a holy God who expects nothing short of perfection and the flawed performance of their own broken lives, Christians can be among the most neurotic people on the planet. Like yo-yos they are up one day but down the next; they are testifying on Sunday but confessing on Monday. Each time they stumble they promise Jesus they will try harder next time but it's no use. They feel like frauds and wonder what will happen to them when their shortcomings are eventually exposed.

The bitter well

The tragedy is that most people in this situation know something is wrong but they think the fault lies with themselves. After all, they are constantly hearing they are not working hard enough. They are told they have got to pray more, give more, fast more, bear more fruit, and while you're at it, how about showing a little more enthusiasm for our latest program? Some Christians are nearly sweating blood for Jesus, and all it's doing is making them sick and tired.

If this is you, the problem is not your effort or desire, it's your gospel. It's contaminated. You're drinking from a poisoned well, and it's making you ill.

The gospel is good news. This is what the word "gospel" literally means: *good news*. By definition, any gospel that leaves you fearful of an angry and judgmental God is no gospel at all. It is not good news. Any gospel that leaves you insecure and uncertain, forever wondering, *Am I accepted? Am I forgiven?* is not good news. Any gospel that demands you sign up for a lifetime of progressive sanctification and yet offers no guarantee that you will ever make it, is not good news. Any gospel that forces cripples to jump through hoops of religious performance is no gospel at all.

The number one reason why many Christians are joyless and tired is because they have never heard the gospel. I know it's hard to believe but it's true—the gospel is almost never preached. Visit any church or switch on the Christian TV channel and chances are you will hear anything and everything *but* the undiluted gospel of the kingdom. Don't blame the preachers. Many of them are doing the best they can, but they can't give what they haven't got, and they can't preach what they haven't heard.

I know of what I speak. I led a church for many years, and every Easter, Christmas, and special invite Sunday I preached the gospel without even knowing what it was. Or rather, I preached what I thought was the gospel but was actually an inferior imitation. My motives were pure, and I had a genuine desire to save the lost, but I was often puzzled why the few people I led to the Lord weren't more joyful. They were earnest (like me), but they weren't exactly bouncing off the ceilings with great joy. Perhaps the angel was wrong about that.

I now realize I was selling a watered-down version of the gospel. I was like the inheritance lawyer handing out windfalls then asking for the money back in taxes and fees. I sold the grace of God on credit. "Buy now, pay later. Sign up today, the first month's free. But once you've settled in we need to talk about personal responsibility, discipleship, and the true cost of following Jesus." I had the right jargon but the wrong theology. It was love with a hook and grace with a price tag.

What madness I preached.

What the gospel is not

What is the gospel? When asked this question people typically respond with a variety of answers. "The gospel is the word of God—it's the scriptures." "It's the story of the Savior as told by Matthew, Mark, Luke, and John." "It's the red-letter teachings of Jesus." "It's God's holy law." "It's an invitation to turn from sin and escape hell." "It's something to believe in no matter what." Although these are common responses, none of them is the gospel.

The scriptures are the gospel truth but they are not *the* gospel. The Bible contains the good news but it also contains much that is not the good news. Unless you know how to tell the difference you're going to be confused when you read it.

The accounts of Matthew, Mark, Luke, and John are called gospels but they are not *the* gospel. Collectively, these four books

4

contain more than 60,000 words but, as we shall see, the gospel can be summarized in a single sentence, even just a word.

The red letters of Jesus are not the gospel. Everything Jesus said was good but not everything he said was good news. Neither was it all meant for you. Jesus preached the law to those who lived under the law on the far side of the cross. We are not under the law but grace (Romans 6:14). We are living under a completely different covenant to the Jews of Jesus' day. Words meant for them are not necessarily meant for you.

The law is not the gospel. The law is good and has its proper purpose but it is bad news not good news. The purpose of the law is to reveal sin and condemn the self-righteous. The bad news of the law silences every mouth and reveals our need for a Savior. The law diagnoses the problem but does nothing to treat it.

The exhortation to "turn from sin" is not the good news. It is not even news. It is an ancient works-oriented message that will leave you sin-focused and introspective. It is the message of Moses and John the Baptist. It is the message of most of the Old Testament. It is not the gospel of grace we find in the New Testament epistles.

Nor is the good news defined as the absence of bad news. Some evangelists think scaring the hell out of people is a good way to win disciples for Jesus, but fear is an appalling basis for any relationship. Jesus is not interested in shotgun weddings. Paul, the greatest church planter in the Bible, preached the gospel without ever mentioning hell by name.

Finally, the gospel is not an article of faith. It is not something that magically springs to life if you believe in it hard enough. It is not the fruit of wishful thinking. Neither is it prophecy. It is not something that will only become real in the future.

The good news is not the good book, the good law, or the good words of the good Teacher. Neither is it good advice, good instruction, or good wishes. The good news is *news* — it is the announcement of the glad tidings of a happy God. The gospel is today's news, and it is unquestionably good.

And now for the news

The gospel is the glad and merry news that God is good, he loves you, and he will happily give up everything he has so he can have you. Contrary to popular belief, God is not mad at you. He is not even in a bad mood. The good news declares that God is happy, he is for you, and he wants to share his life with you forever.[2]

Jesus is proof of this. The veracity of the gospel is evidenced in his death and resurrection. On the cross God showed that he loved us while we were sinners and that he would rather die than live without us. And through the resurrection he proved that nothing — not even death — can separate us from the love that is ours in Jesus Christ.

Through our representative Jesus our heavenly Father has joined himself to us, promising never to leave nor forsake us. We stand secure, not on our feeble promises to him, but on his unconditional and unbreakable promises to us.

And that's it: God loves you and wants to be with you. It's simple but it's the biggest truth in the universe. We will spend eternity discovering in a billion different ways the limitless expressions of his unending love. Indeed, this is what we were made for — to receive and respond to his divine love. This is the fundamental law of our existence and the reason for our being. This is the best news you ever heard.

The love-gift

The gospel is so simple that it's hard for our grown-up minds to grasp. *It can't be that good. There must be a catch.* Before I understood the simplicity of the gospel, my mind was like an ashtray — full of "buts." *God loves you but … Jesus died for you but …* As I understood it, God's gifts always come with a price tag. Only they don't. They can't. Don't you see? Grace must be free or it's not grace. Don't let anyone charge you for what God has freely given.

The gospel that Jesus preached begins like this: "For God so loved that he gave …" The gospel is first and foremost a declaration of love backed up with a gift. It's the announcement of a love-gift and the gift is Jesus. Right here is where many miss it. They

6

take the greatest gift in the universe, put it inside a little box called "my salvation," and then put that box in the cupboard of their past.

"The gospel? Oh that's for sinners. I've heard it. I'm saved. I have no further use for it."

The angel would disagree with you. The angel said the gospel is for all people, saint and sinner alike. Salvation is one of the many benefits of the gospel, but there is more to this gift than salvation. Jesus is not only the Savior, he is *God with us*. Our minds can barely begin to unpack the significance of this revelation. *God is with us*. He is not up there but down here. He is not against us but for us. If he has already given us his Son, what will he withhold from us? Wow! This is Grand Canyon theology. This is the gospel that takes your breath away leaving you speechless in marveling adoration. *He will never leave or abandon us*. What relief! What peace! This is green pastures beside still waters. This is home. This is our rest.

The gospel is bigger and better than you think. The goodness of the good news is directly proportional to the goodness of God and the newsiness of the good news is proportional to the level of revelation we have about him. Since God is infinitely good and infinitely big, and since there is always more for us to discover about him, there is always more to the good news than we can ever think or imagine. The gospel is simple but it gets bigger and better on closer examination until your mind is fried and you are floored with gratitude at the loving-kindness of a good God.

Spurgeon's nail

What is the gospel? It is the revelation of God's love through Jesus Christ. Whatever your need, your answer is found in Christ alone. He is the Love who loves us and the Grace who helps us in our time of need. If you are a sinner in need of redemption, see Jesus. If you are a saint struggling with sin, see Jesus. If you are oppressed by poverty, you don't need a sermon outlining seven steps to prosperity—you need a revelation of Jesus, who became poor for our sakes so that we might be rich (2 Corinthians 8:9). If you are facing a storm and don't know the way forward, you need a revelation of the One who silenced the tempest with a word. If you are looking for a solution to one of the world's many problems, Jesus has it. Since Jesus is the author of life, he is the first and last word on any and every subject.

When I started pastoring I saw needs everywhere, and I tailored my preaching to suit. If there was sin in the camp I preached on repentance and why you should do it. Then I preached on holiness and how to attain it. I was a Whack-A-Mole preacher. Whenever a problem popped up, I would thump it with my Bible. Foolishly, I thought my homiletic skills combined with my profound understanding of scripture would solve everyone's problems. In truth, it was a recipe for powerless preaching, carnal Christianity, and boring church. (If you were there, forgive me.)

Then I discovered a profound truth. You can know the Bible from cover to cover and not know the gospel. Read the written word through any lens other than the Living Word and you'll end up with a counterfeit gospel and lifeless religion. When the scales fell from my eyes, my first reaction was shock—*how had I missed this?*—followed by unbridled joy—*God, you're even better than I thought!* I began to see Jesus on every single page of my Bible. *It's all about him!* I burned all my sermon notes and started again. I began to preach Jesus and nothing else. In this regard I was channeling Spurgeon who said this in 1891:

> I sometimes wonder that you do not get tired of my preaching, because I do nothing but hammer away on this one nail. I have driven it in up to the head, and I have gone round to the other side to clinch it; but still I keep at it. With me it is, year after year, "None but Jesus! None but Jesus!" Oh, you great saints, if you have outgrown the need of a sinner's trust in the Lord Jesus, you have outgrown your sins, but you have also outgrown your grace, and your saintship has ruined you.[3]

I was saved for thirty-four years before I began to see the gospel in all its liberating glory. I was well on my way to becoming a ruined saint, encaged by my own and other people's expectations.

But the windows of my soul were opened, and I breathed again the fresh air of heaven. I will never go back into that cage.

Freedom for all

The gospel is good news for the prisoner, both saved and unsaved. If you are feeling the deadweight yoke of sin or huffing-puffing piety, the gospel will set you free. Just like that. There is power in the gospel like you cannot imagine. I've seen decades-old burdens and ancient wounds broken in a moment. I've seen dead sinners raised to new life and decrepit saints given fresh legs. It's like the Holy Spirit is waiting for us to say "Yes" to grace and when we do, *Pow!* — freedom comes and we are changed.

In contrast with the dead religion of man, the living gospel of grace is totally supernatural.

But here's the important part. The one thing that can stop you from walking in the love and grace of God is your own dismissive incredulity and unbelief. I am not talking about atheism; unbelief comes in subtler shades. In the church unbelief is manifested in the faithless language of debt and obligation. It's asking God to do what he's already done. It's trying to impersonate Jesus. It's bringing sacrifices and offerings he has not asked for.

This is not the way you receive a gift.

The gospel is true whether you believe it or not, but it won't do you any good unless you believe it. No one is going to force you to leave the jungle. The sole condition for receiving God's gift of grace is you have to want it. The sinner must drop his guns and the saint must put down her offerings so that both may come with empty hands and faith-filled hearts to the table of his blessings.

The only thing that can render worthless the exceeding riches of God's grace is unbelief. Unbelief prays, "God, please do this, and that, and the other thing," but faith looks to the finished work of the cross and says, "Lord, you have done it all." Unbelief gives — "Lord, look at what I've done/built/brought for you" — but faith receives — "Look at what you have done for us." Unbelief toils and accomplishes nothing; faith understands that everything comes to us by grace for free. Unbelief tries but faith trusts.

Jake's story

As I was writing this prologue I received a message from a young man I will call Jake. Jake wrote to tell me he loved God and wanted a relationship with him but didn't know what to do or how to be saved. He said he had heard from some religious people that God expects us to live a sinless life and that he won't approve of us if we go out dancing with friends and that sort of thing.

At this point you may be thinking, "How misguided, dancing is not a sin." I know, it's laughable. But don't miss the bigger issue. Christianity isn't a list of do's and don'ts. Christianity is Christ. The point is not whether dancing is on your *do list* or your *don't list*; the point is whether you have any list at all. Rule-minded people are preoccupied with doing good and avoiding evil but this is carnal religion. It's eating from the wrong tree. Christianity isn't a test, it's a rest.

So here's Jake listening to the bad news of religion telling him God won't accept him unless he first sorts himself out and changes his behavior. I hope you can see that this is not good news. In fact, charging sinners admission to the throne of grace is a fiendish practice. But I'm getting ahead of myself.

What really struck me was Jake's claim that this bad news message was "what I have heard my whole life." Jake sounded like he had some church experience and he clearly loved the Lord, but no one had ever told him the good news.

Don't you find it astonishing that with all the churches in the world and wall-to-wall Christian television, there are millions if not billions of people just like Jake who have never heard the gospel? I hear from people like this every single day.

Since no one had ever told Jake the gospel, the privilege of proclaiming that happy message fell to me. In a few short sentences I told him that God loves him and there is nothing he can do to make God love him any more than he already does. I explained that going to church and avoiding sin would not save him, and the only thing that pleases God is faith in his Son Jesus. "If you would be saved, you need to trust that Jesus is who he said he is, that he loves you, died for you, and now lives for you." I then encouraged

Jake to talk to God directly and ask him to reveal his love. Within an hour I received the following reply:

> Wow, that sure is good news. I would say that is great news! Thank you so much. I had no clue that's what Jesus is really about.

Two days later Jake wrote again to tell me he was now saved, he had been talking to God and God was helping him a great deal. Now that's what you call effortless evangelism. I simply passed along the good news, the Holy Spirit brought revelation and Jake was set free.

And not one mole was whacked.

The short and sweet gospel

History's greatest preachers have always proclaimed a simple gospel with few words and much power.

Paul brought the kingdom of heaven to the pagan city of Corinth with nothing more than a five-word gospel—"Jesus Christ and him crucified"—backed up with the power of the Holy Spirit.

Peter needed only twelve words to declare to his fellow Jews the good news: "God has made this Jesus, whom you crucified, both Lord and Christ." Three thousand believed and were saved the same day.

John needed only seven words to herald the end of the old covenant and the dawn of the new: "Grace and truth came through Jesus Christ."

And Jesus needed just nine words to reveal himself as the end of all our searching: "I am the way, the truth, and the life."[4]

As you can see, there are many different ways of saying the same thing. As long as you are revealing the love of God as personified by Jesus—who he is, what he has done and why—then you are preaching the gospel.

This should not be complicated. The gospel is simple enough for a child to understand. You don't need to know Greek to get it. Neither do you need to go to seminary or Bible school to figure it all out.

One of my favorite gospels is this twenty-word gem which was probably first uttered by John Calvin: "The Son of God became the Son of Man that the sons of men might become the sons of God." Short and sweet.

Or how about this shorter gospel by Anna Bartlett Warner: "Jesus loves me this I know, for the Bible tells me so."[5] That's the gospel my three-year-old son knows.

Here is the gospel we sing at Christmas:

Veiled in flesh the Godhead see; hail the incarnate Deity,
Pleased with us in flesh to dwell, Jesus our Emmanuel ...
Mild he lays his glory by, born that man no more may die,
Born to raise the sons of earth, born to give them second birth.

That's from "Hark! The Herald Angels Sing" if you haven't made the connection. Charles Wesley's 270-year-old hymn proves the best gospels are enduring. They stick in our hearts because they speak to our deepest needs and remind us of our true home.

Of course you don't need to be a gifted hymn writer or preacher to have a short gospel. Some time ago I challenged readers of my blog, Escape to Reality, to proclaim the good news in as few words as possible.[6]

Steve from Sydney supplied this short gospel: "Receive Christ and you will be as clean as he is, as free as he is, and as close as he is to the Father God."

Phil from Alabama gave us his ten-word gospel: "Jesus loves you and God is not mad at you."

Daniel from Massachusetts provided a nine-word gospel: "Come! The sin barrier is down. I love you."

And Miriam from Nebraska gave us this stunning nine-word affirmation: "In God's family forever by his work and power."

Some say that a tsunami of grace is currently sweeping across the world. If this is so, then one of the signs of this grace awakening will be an increasing emphasis on the short and simple gospel Jesus revealed and the New Testament writers proclaimed.

The gospel of grace is wholly unlike the rule-based religion many of us are familiar with. Religion is complicated but grace is simple. Religion is vague but grace is crystal clear. Religion finds fault and does nothing to help, but the grace of God propels you triumphantly through life's toughest challenges. Religion will give you a headache and leave you sick and tired, but grace gives strength to the weary and life to the dead. Religion seeks to bridle the free but grace liberates the prisoner and the oppressed.

It is my firm conviction that as more people come to appreciate the beauty and richness of the undiluted gospel, sermons on other subjects will disappear like yesterday's news. The power of God is only revealed in the gospel, and we have been called to preach nothing less.

Pictures at an exhibition

If the gospel is short, why have I written a whole book about it? For the same reason miners dig deep holes in the sides of mountains — there's treasure inside. The gospel reveals not only a door into the King's domain but the lobby, the grounds, and the entire realm of his splendor.

The blessings of the gospel are many but in this book we are going to look at just ten. These ten blessings should not be interpreted as levels or steps or anything like that. Instead, think of them as pearls on a necklace or pictures at an exhibition. They are riffs on the theme of Jesus. They are ten revelations of grace that describe the life of every believer, no exceptions. In union with Christ you are loved, forgiven, saved, accepted, holy, righteous, dead to sin, new, and royal.

As I came to the end of writing this book a friend asked me about the title. "Are you aware that 'the ten words' is another name for the Ten Commandments?" I was not aware and his question prompted a moment of panic. *Oh no. People will think this book is based on the law. That's hardly a good look for a preacher of grace!*

I began to wonder if I had made a mistake with the title but my friend disagreed. "It's a good thing and not a coincidence." He was right. God knows I love lists and I'm certain he was the one who gave me the idea for the book and the title. So I decided to keep the title unchanged.

Then that night, a confirmation. Camilla and I were watching an episode of *The West Wing* and President Bartlett was on a quest for a sound bite. "Ten words, ten words!" came the call from the Oval Office. "We're still looking for ten words," said his chief of staff. Not nine, not eleven, but ten words. It's like my favorite fictional president was saying, "You picked a great title."

So it's *The Gospel in Ten Words* — not nine, not eleven, but ten. You've heard the ten words of God's law; now receive the ten words of his grace.

Yet in a way, the title of this book is misleading. You don't need ten words to get the gospel, you just need one and that word is Jesus. The gospel is not *Jesus-plus-you* or *Jesus-plus-whatever-doctrine-is-in-vogue*. It's just Jesus. His is the only name by which we can receive forgiveness and acceptance and holiness and all the other manifestations of grace I have written about in this book. Don't ever forget that. (I'll quiz you at the end of the book to make sure you haven't.)

Before we enter the gallery of his grace, let us give one final thought to Lieutenant Onoda of the Japanese Army. After he was finally convinced the Pacific War had ended, he became a different man. He stopped terrorizing the Filipino farmers and set up a generous scholarship fund for their children. He later returned to the Philippines to thank the people for their assistance in keeping him alive during his self-imposed isolation.[7]

Just as Lieutenant Onoda became a different man after he accepted the good news of war's end, I trust you will be a different person by the time you reach the end of this book. The gospel changes us. It delivers us from who we were and empowers us to be who we were always meant to be. It does this not by giving us instructions or telling us what to do but by revealing the true nature of God. I guarantee that when you see the God behind the gospel, you will never be the same again.

It is my prayer that as you read this book you will be led gently by the Spirit out of whatever jungle you may be in and that you will begin to dance freely on the wide open spaces of God's amazing grace. Whether you are a young sinner or an old saint, I hope that as you encounter the grace of God on these pages you will come face to face with Jesus himself.

Jesus is the Good News!

For God so loved the world that he gave his one and only Son ...
(John 3:16)

"So, what did you learn in Sunday school, Sweetie?" We were driving home from church and my question was directed to my six-year-old daughter.

"We learned about the Ten Commandments."

"Did you now? Tell me something — will God love you more if you keep the Ten Commandments?"

There was a long pause in the back seat. My daughter could smell a trap. "Er, yes?" she said hesitantly.

"No," I replied. "God loves you when you're good, and he loves you when you're naughty. He loves you all the time. Just like me," I added with a smile.

Like most parents, I love my kids regardless of their behavior. If my little girl was to grow up and break all Ten Commandments, she would still be my little girl and I would love her dearly. Yet many think God is not as loving as we are. They have been taught that his love is filtered through an anger management problem. "Sure, God loves you, but he's also mad at you. So you'd better watch yourself." Just as it's rare to hear sermons on the unmixed gospel, seldom do you hear the love of God preached without hooks and qualifications. It's unconditional love — with conditions.

How is it that we think we love our kids more than God loves us?

Love greater than mountains

God is not mad with you. He loves you with an everlasting love. Though the mountains be shaken and the hills depart, his unfailing love for you will not be removed (Isaiah 54:10).

You may ask, "But what about those verses on God's anger?"

Do you mean the ones that say his anger is momentary but his love is everlasting?[1] I love them. They are a great comfort to me.

God was angry at your sin, in the same way I might get angry at the sicknesses that afflict my children, but he dealt with your sin once and for all 2,000 years ago. On the cross the One who knew no sin became sin on your behalf so that sin might be utterly condemned in him (Romans 8:3). Taking the sin of the world into his body, Jesus drank from the cup of God's wrath and he drank that cup dry. His grace is greater than your sin.

The cross is a picture of spent anger and furious love. The cross is God shouting, "Let my children go!" We can barely fathom this. We had done nothing to merit his favor. From the very beginning we had rejected his overtures and sold our love to a slaver. And when he showed up to help us we killed him. But on the cross our True Love ransomed us and set us free.

> But God demonstrates his own love for us in this: While we were still sinners, Christ died for us. (Romans 5:8)

God showed us his great love while we were sinners. He did not wait for us to get cleaned up or repent or make a fresh start. While we were in the filth of our sin and self-righteousness he came and hugged us.

How can you qualify such relentless love? How can you say, "God loves you but ..."? There are no buts. The love of God is not buttressed by buts. It is measureless and so incomprehensibly vast our minds cannot grasp it. We can't apprehend it because human love is unlike divine love.

Earthly, human love is a response to loveliness, but divine love is spontaneous, arising in and of itself. God does not love us because we are lovely but because he is love. It is his nature to love us. Since God always acts in accordance with his nature, his wrath, along with everything else he does, should be seen as an expression of his love. Why does God do what he does? Because he is love and he loves us. Love is his motive for everything.

16

1. Loved

Unfallen love

Human love bears the marks of the fall but God's love is untainted, unfailing, and unconditional. Through the prophet Jeremiah he assures us:

> I've never quit loving you and never will. Expect love, love, and more love! (Jeremiah 31:3b, The Message)

Unlike brittle human love, God's love "bears all things, believes all things, hopes all things, endures all things" (1 Corinthians 13:7, NKJV). His love will never wear out or die. Human love is fickle but God's love is constant. It is the bedrock of the universe and the reason you are here. It is no exaggeration to say that God loves you with the white-hot intensity of a thousand suns. Just look at the night sky. He put those stars there to impress you with the astronomical extravagance of his love. God loved you into existence and he loved you when you were a sinner. His heart's desire is for you to know and enjoy his love for eternity.

Do these words move you? When you reflect on his love does it fill your soul with sunshine? Many people get it but only a little bit. In their minds the love of God is like the weather on Alpha Centauri. "Yes, I'm sure it's amazing, I'm just not aware of it." To them, the love of God is like the love of a king for his subjects—formal, distant, and aloof. Like Job, they are ignorant of God's love:

> Oh, Job, don't you see how God's wooing you from the jaws of danger? How he's drawing you into wide-open places—inviting you to feast at a table laden with blessings? (Job 36:16, The Message)

Job was a pious and decent man but he was also a fearful believer in karma. He made a habit of buying spiritual insurance through his frequent sacrifices and offerings in the hope that his good deeds would ameliorate any bad deeds done by his family. When things went well Job took the credit. "My good deeds must be paying off." But when things went pear-shaped he was lost and perplexed. "What have I done to deserve this?"

17

Job was so focused on himself and his merits he was oblivious to the love of God. If Job and his sacrifices are a picture of superstitious religion, then his friend Elihu is the gospel preacher: "Stop what you are doing and consider the wonders of God" (see Job 37:14). See the stars. Hear the rolling thunder. Walk through the woods and look down from lofty mountain grandeur. The universe declares that God is good and that he cares for you.

For us on this side of Calvary there is no greater wonder than the cross. Job's religion of sacrifices and offerings says you must do this and that to merit God's love, but the cross demolishes all such nonsense at a stroke. The cross declares that God is good and that he cares for you. The cross is the cure for any doubts you may have about the love of God.

To the modern-day Job, Elihu might say:

> Stop and consider the wonder of the cross. Don't you see how God is wooing you from trouble into security, from the impoverished famine of your own life to the rich feast of his? This is not a reward for your sacrifices and offerings; this is the good news of his grace and favor.

not by works, but by grace & faith

Love that stoops

Religious types get nervy whenever the gospel of grace is brought up. They worry that this "latest fad," this "new teaching," will lead people into dangerous places. Well, if the love of God is a dangerous place, there is no better place to be because that is exactly where grace will take you.

God is love and love that stoops is called grace. The gospel of grace is really the gospel of his love. Grace is what God's love looks like from our side. Grace is love come down.

An illustration may help. I love my kids with all my heart but I live in a different world to them. The things I enjoy are above their understanding. So if they are to know my love, one of two things must happen: either they must come up, or I must go down. Since I am their father, I take the initiative. I go down. I choose to engage with them at their level: to get on the floor and wrestle with them; to read them stories I would never read myself; to play and tickle and push their trikes until I'm spent. This is love in action and every parent knows it.

This is exactly how God loves us. He does not love us like a king but a father. This is the supreme revelation of Jesus who is grace personified. God came down that we might go up. Jesus became like us so that we might become like him — whole, healthy, blessed, and completely secure in his Father's love.

In the greatest parable ever told, Jesus revealed that God is like a father watching for your return, who runs when he sees you coming, and who falls on you with hugs and kisses. You may come with your prepared speech, your good intentions, and a desire to serve but he's not interested in any of that. He just wants you.

Love looks like grace. When you receive his grace you receive his love. There is no difference. This means if you have no time for grace, perhaps because you are striving to please the Lord with your sacrifices and offerings, then you have no time for love. Reject grace and you reject love. — it is not painful but learned

Learning to walk in the love of God means learning to walk in his grace. It's following Jesus instead of Job. It's no longer trying to impress God with your sacrifices but being impressed with his.

God will never make you jump through hoops to earn his love. He won't love you any more if you succeed and he won't love you any less if you fail. If you lead millions to Christ or none at all, he will love you just the same. God loved you while you were dead in sin and he didn't stop loving you when you got saved. His love endures forever.[2]

The gospel of grace is no new teaching or passing fad. It is as ancient and eternal as the love of God itself.

The law doesn't love you

So much for Job; what about Moses? Under the old covenant you loved God because you had to; it was the law. But love doesn't work that way. Love cannot be legislated; that was the whole point of the command. The law was not given to manufacture love among the loveless but to reveal our need for a Lover.

From the beginning, God desired a relationship with us but we preferred rules. God told the Israelites that he wanted them to be his treasured people but they weren't interested. Their attitude was, "Just tell us what to do and we'll do it."

The reason some prefer the clear-cut rules of religion to the confusing freedom of relationship is because they do not know they are God's dearly loved children. They are fearful and look to the rules to give them the security and identity we all need. The religious spirit panders to this fear by saying, "Do this and don't do that and just maybe God will be pleased with you." This message may be sold as "Four keys to pleasing God" or "Seven steps to intimacy," but it's actually child abuse. It is putting a price tag on the affection that is already ours by right of sonship.

A preference for the rules is a surefire sign that one is not standing secure in the love of God. Consider the Pharisees; they were big on rules. They preached religious duty and obligation and were keen missionaries who would travel over land and sea to win a single convert. Yet Jesus said to them, "You do not have the love of God in your hearts" (John 5:42). This is why we must never listen to the lies religion teaches about love. Religion cannot give you what religion does not have.

The Israelites' preference for rules over relationship is one of history's great tragedies. Yet their choice is repeated every day by sincere people who think they have to keep the commandments to be loved, saved, or blessed. Although the law covenant went out the window 2,000 years ago they didn't get the memo. They are trying to love God because they think they are supposed to. Instead of basking in the light of his divine love they are trying to produce light on their own. The problem is they can't do it. They are like a moon trying to be a sun.

Love in Ephesus

I am reminded of the Ephesians who left their first love. The Ephesian believers had faith and they had deeds, and if you had asked them I'm sure they would have boldly declared their love *for* Christ. Yet Paul prayed they would know the love *of* Christ (Ephesians 3:14–19). See the difference? Our love goes up but

20

more important is the love that comes down. We love because he first loved us, and he loved us because he is love. Love is a noun before it's a verb.

When you know the love of God, when you begin to realize just Who loves you and how committed he is to your success, it gives you confidence. Your faith is energized and you begin to release his love to those around you. Life becomes a supernatural adventure. But lose sight of his love and faith is diminished. You become what Paul would call a "mere man" (1 Corinthians 3:4). When that happens, anything that requires love—marriage, parenting, working with people—becomes a chore.

Something like this happened to the Ephesians. They got so busy with their church work they drifted from their first love. Jesus had to come and correct them (Revelation 2:1–7). Who is our first love? It's him! He is the light. He is the source. He is the Sun that rides above all shadows.

The Ephesians were famous for their deeds yet Jesus basically said to them, "Stop what you're doing. Remember the height from which you have fallen and do the things you did at first." What were the things they did at first? Probably not much. I led a church for ten years and at the beginning we did little. We had no programs to keep us busy, no teams to manage, no leaders to train, no battles to fight, no website to maintain, and no vision to implement. What did we do with all our free time? We lived loved; we loved God, we loved each other, and we looked for ways to love our neighbors. True, my understanding of God's grace was a little mixed up, but we knew how to sit at the feet of Jesus and receive his love. Later, as the church began to grow, we got busy sometimes to the point of distraction. But in the beginning we were more Mary than Martha.

Mary's choice is the key to successful living. Unlike busy Martha, Mary chose the one thing that is needed: receiving from Jesus the love that looks like grace.

Most of us know the Mary and Martha story as told in Luke 10, but we don't know what happened next. I like to think Mary went on to accomplish great things. Just as children who are raised in loving homes tend to succeed in life, I'll bet Mary did great exploits. Maybe she raised healthy kids or planted a church or became a seven-term mayor. I have no idea. But the odds of success were high. God had come into her living room, looked her in the eye and loved on her. How could she fail?

Be imitators of God, therefore, as dearly loved children. (Ephesians 5:1)

HE > i

Like Mary, Paul also knew a thing or two about the love of God. He understood there is no such thing as success outside of his love. "If I move mountains but have not love, I am nothing" (see 1 Corinthians 13:2). Yes, there is work to be done and a harvest to be gathered. But we do none of these things to earn God's affection or approval. We do it because we are his dearly loved children and we want to be about our Daddy's business.

Better than life

Living in Asia I had plenty of friends who were poor missionaries. Many of those who were ultimately successful had stories like this:

> I came to the end of my resources, I was at my wit's end, and I didn't know what to do. In desperation I begged God to provide. Instead, he flooded my soul with the vast affection of his love. I heard him say, "I love you," and in an instant everything changed. Suddenly nothing else mattered. The unpaid bills became inconsequential. The problems that had been hanging over my head like anvils became trivial. I had been set free by a profound revelation. *My heavenly Father loves me!* How could I fail? Whether I lived or died, it did not matter because I knew my Daddy is for me.

Have you ever experienced the love of God in the middle of a crisis? There is nothing like it. It leaves you dancing on the waves of uncertainty and scoffing at the storm of your circumstances.

Have you ever experienced the love of God in the middle of a decision? It leaves you grinning like a winner knowing that whatever you choose you will win, even if your choice is fatal. I know, in the natural it doesn't make sense. But who wants to live in the natural? I much prefer the superior realm of his love.

How does God woo us from the jaws of distress? By having us drink from the boundless oceans of his love, by drawing us into the sunlit fields of his grace, and by preparing a table laden with blessings in the presence of our enemies. God invariably deals with our problems by giving us a greater revelation of himself and his love. Our part is to choose whether we will continue to operate in the inferior reality of our circumstances or walk in the higher reality of his love. This choice is the difference between success and failure.

I am who I am

Mary's choice and Paul's choice and the choice of every successful son or daughter of God is the choice to live loved. It is saying, "World, you cannot pressure me. Your carrots and sticks mean nothing to me. I run on the love of God, and when I feel his pleasure, boy, do I run!"

A revelation of God's lavish love is transformational. It will resurrect a dead marriage, heal a broken family, and rocket your ministry onto a trajectory to who-knows-where-but-it-doesn't-matter-because-it's-Papa's-business-and-I'm-just-thrilled-to-come-along-for-the-ride.

Love is not just the first chapter in a book on the gospel; love is life. In fact, the love of God is better than life. If I had to choose between my life and his love I would take his love every time, for it is only in his love that we truly live.

Your One Big Truth and the wisdom of Puddleglum

Lately I have been asking myself, "What is the one supreme lesson I want my kids to learn from me?" In other words, what is my One Big Truth? Your One Big Truth is your answer to this question: What is the most important lesson I have learned in life? Your One Big Truth is the truth you cling to when all is lost. It's the backbone that helps you stand and the keel that keeps you on course. It's the spark in your imagination, the drive in your engine, and the peace in your sleep.

Perhaps you have never thought about this before. Then consider Puddleglum the Marsh-wiggle. Puddleglum is one of my favorite characters from *The Chronicles of Narnia*. He is grim, gloomy, and famously pessimistic, but he's a good wiggle in a storm. If you have read *The Silver Chair* by C. S. Lewis, you will know what I'm talking about.

Near the end of that story, Puddleglum and his friends, Jill and Eustace, find themselves trapped in the dark, subterranean world of Underland. An evil enchantress tries to convince them the world they are looking for does not exist. Aided by incense and music she weaves a web of lies making out that Narnia is nothing but a make-believe world and its king, Aslan, a foolish dream. Jill and Eustace begin to fall under her influence but steadfast Puddleglum breaks the spell with a bold declaration:

> Suppose we have only dreamed, or made up all those things ... Suppose this black pit of a kingdom of yours is the only world. Well, it strikes me as a pretty poor one ... That's why I'm going to stand by the play-world. I'm on Aslan's side even if there isn't any Aslan to lead it. I'm going to live as like a Narnian as I can even if there isn't any Narnia.[3]

Puddleglum's One Big Truth was that Aslan and Narnia were more real than the world he could see with his eyes. Acting on his conviction, Puddleglum refuted the witch's lies, stomped on her evil-smelling fire, and saved the day.

As Puddleglum so brilliantly shows us, your One Big Truth is an undimmable light in a dark world. It is an unbreakable bridge between where you are and where you need to be. If Puddleglum had not been so sure of his One Big Truth, all would have been lost. It is unlikely he and his friends would have escaped the realm of Underland.

So what is your One Big Truth? What is your central belief?

In my travels I have encountered several beliefs that people have adopted as their Big Truths. Some say it is obedience: "The most important thing is to obey God no matter what." Others say it is attitude: "The main thing is to make a good effort; God knows your heart." Still others say it is sacrifice: "Give God your best; he has already given you so much" — or fruit: "Prove yourself as his disciple."

The difficulty I have with beliefs such as these is that they rely on *me* — my obedience, my attitude, my sacrifice, and my fruit-bearing — and I just don't have that much faith in me. Like Puddleglum, my faith is in another. My backbone comes from someone else. My faith is in God

So what is my One Big Truth? It is this: God loves us with an unfailing love. This is simply mind-blowing to me. Every form of love you and I will experience in this world is *failing* love — it breaks and it bruises, it disappoints and ultimately it dies. But God's love *never, ever* fails. Not ever. Not even death can stop his love. Why do I believe in the resurrection? Because God says he loves us with an everlasting love.[4] Everlasting means everlasting. Either God has to raise you from the dead and keep on loving you or else he is a liar. God is not a liar. His love for you will never wear out or die. Cancer can't keep you from his love. Neither can depression, AIDs, or alcoholism. The devil and all his demons cannot separate you from his love. Neither can death nor life. The only thing that can come between you and his love is your refusal to receive it. The only thing that can separate you from the love of God is you. I choose to live in God's love

Knowing the Father's love

Think of the prodigal son. His father loved him the same at the beginning of the story as at the end. His love was without shadow or variation. But the prodigal didn't *know* his father's love until he was embraced. I am sure the father wanted to hug his son every day but the son wasn't interested — not at first. The older brother didn't know his father's love either. His One Big Truth was based on his obedience: "All these years I have been slaving for you and never disobeyed your orders." If the younger brother was a rebel, then the older brother was a right-living, religious man. But neither son knew his father's love. Neither had allowed the father to fall on them in that bear-like embrace of unrestrained love.

The love of God is transformational but it will not change you unless you know it in your heart. The truth doesn't set you free; it

with a never ending love

is knowing and being convinced about the truth that sets you free. You need to let God love you the way he wants to love you. You need to let him fall on you as he fell on those in the upper room. Pentecost was not primarily an encounter with God's power; it was an encounter with his powerful, transforming love. The apostles were filled with the Holy Spirit who is the Spirit of love.[5]

God's love changes us. It turns sinners into saints and haters into lovers. Just look at Paul. When he met Love personified he became a different man. Like the disciple "whom Jesus loved," Paul experienced a love that was personal and intimate, causing him to write of the One "who loved *me* and gave himself for *me*" (Galatians 2:20).

do you know God's love!

What about you? Can you say, like Paul, that "God loves *me*"? Do you know his love? When you think of God do you see him as a distant king or your loving Papa? When you consider his gaze toward you is he frowning or smiling?

I promised myself when I started this book that I would stick to the gospel — just proclaim it and move on. But I have to pause here a moment and play the preacher. Permit me to ask you an important question. Do you know that God loves you? Are you convinced he loves you when you're good and when you're bad, when you're up and when you're down, when you succeed and when you stumble? Do you believe he loves you for richer or poorer, in sickness and in health, and that death won't ever do you part?

Perhaps you have been following Job the sacrifice-bringer or Moses the law-keeper in a futile attempt to merit the love and favor of God. If so, heed the words of Elihu and Jesus: "Stop what you are doing." Stop trusting in your sacrifices and good deeds, and consider the wonders of God as revealed in Christ and his work. Look to the cross and see the fierce and furious love of God in action. Don't ever doubt that he loves you — *yes you!* — with an unfailing love. His love for you is stronger than the bond between a mother and her nursing baby (Isaiah 49:15). You are his dearly loved child. So stop striving and settle yourself in his arms of love. Make him your place of repose and abide in his love.

we don't only go to God "when we need him" but live in communion with Him always

26

The gospel of love

The gospel of grace declares that God's love is greater than your sin and that there is nothing you can do to earn it. All you can do is receive it by faith.

Carnal religion would have you believe that God is standing with crossed arms, but grace declares his arms are always open. Religion says God is angry and maybe hates you, but grace proclaims he is always in a good mood and his favor rests upon you. Religion says you need to get yourself sorted out and cleaned up before you can come home, but grace shouts, "Come now, just as you are!"

There has only ever been one place to find the unconditional love all of us need, and that place is revealed in the good news. The gospel is not a solicitation to impress God with your love. The gospel is the passionate declaration of your Father's undying love for you. Everything in the gospel—his forgiveness, acceptance, and righteousness—is good and true because your heavenly Father loves you. He always has and he always will. God never changes.

I write to you, dear children, because your sins have been forgiven
on account of his name. (1 John 2:12)

F O R G I V E N

I get asked more questions about forgiveness than any other
subject. "Am I really forgiven? What if I sin and don't repent?
What if I backslide?" Forgiveness seems to be a blind spot for
many people. We just can't get it into our heads that God has
forgiven us completely and for all time. "That just sounds too
good to be true. Nothing comes for free. There must be a price to
pay." There was – and Jesus paid it.

The grace of God has many expressions but forgiveness is one
of the biggest. Miss forgiveness and you'll miss grace. So one way
to set aside grace is to treat forgiveness as something other than a
gift. Sadly, many do. They think they have to do certain things
before God will forgive them. They think this way because of
something Jesus said and something John said.

Bad news sold as good news

Jesus said, "If you do not forgive men their sins, your Father will
not forgive your sins" (Matthew 6:15). This is not good news. This
is bad news that should make us shake in our boots for it links
God's forgiveness to our own. It is not grace, it is law. It is quid
pro quo and tit for tat. It is something you must give to get.

Why did the Lord of grace preach law? Because some people
will never value the gift of grace until the law has been allowed to
do its condemning work. Some people need to hear the bad news
before they will appreciate the good news.

Jesus said he came to fulfill the law and on the cross he did
exactly that. In the act of paying for the world's sin, he forgave
those who had sinned against him. See the connection? The very
condition for forgiveness that Jesus preached on the mount, he

himself satisfied on the cross. Now Christ is the end of the law for all who trust in him (Romans 10:4).

Perhaps you have heard that "God won't forgive you if you are harboring unforgiveness in your heart." Under the law that Jesus preached, that was true. But the law-keeping covenant was fulfilled at the cross. Those who maintain we must forgive to be forgiven are confused about the finished work of Calvary. They will draw your attention to those scriptures that say forgiveness is conditional while ignoring those that say it isn't.

We need to have a whole Bible theology but that does not mean "read everything indiscriminately and hope for the best." That would be like going to the drug cabinet and swallowing every pill in sight. A whole Bible theology means you read the written word through the lens of the Living Word. It means you filter everything you read through Christ and his finished work on the cross.

Look at the figure below and you will see a consistent pattern of preaching conditional forgiveness prior to the cross and unconditional forgiveness after the cross. Before the cross Jesus preached forgiveness as a law to be kept; after the cross he said it was a gift to be received (Acts 26:18). The cross really did change everything.

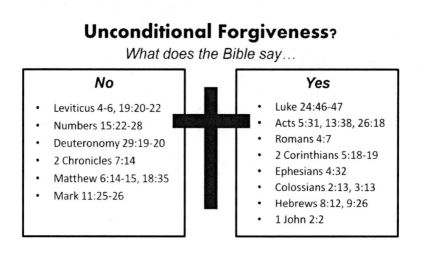

Unconditional Forgiveness?
What does the Bible say...

No		Yes
• Leviticus 4-6, 19:20-22		• Luke 24:46-47
• Numbers 15:22-28		• Acts 5:31, 13:38, 26:18
• Deuteronomy 29:19-20		• Romans 4:7
• 2 Chronicles 7:14		• 2 Corinthians 5:18-19
• Matthew 6:14-15, 18:35		• Ephesians 4:32
• Mark 11:25-26		• Colossians 2:13, 3:13
		• Hebrews 8:12, 9:26
		• 1 John 2:2

New covenant nouns

On the day he rose from the dead, Jesus immediately began to preach a different message from the law-based sermons he had delivered before the cross. Recall that before the cross Jesus preached conditional forgiveness; forgive to be forgiven. But after the cross he preached this:

the law is complete and grace has come

> This is what is written: The Christ will suffer and rise from the dead on the third day, and *repentance (and) for-giveness* of sins will be preached in his name to all nations, beginning at Jerusalem. (Luke 24:46–47)

not for but and

Now take a moment to go and check that passage in your own Bible. What does it say? Does it say "repentance *for* forgiveness" or "repentance *and* forgiveness"? The difference is huge. Repentance for forgiveness is what John the Baptist preached. It's forgiveness conditional on you turning from sin. It's a verb for a verb.

But this is not what Jesus is saying here. He doesn't use verbs for repentance and forgiveness but nouns.[1] He's saying, "From now on, forgiveness is not something God does, it's something he's *done*."

This becomes clear when we read the verse in the King James Bible:

> Repentance and remission of sins should be preached in his name among all nations, beginning at Jerusalem. (Luke 24:47, KJV)

we are already forgiven

Forgiveness that has taken place is called remission. When were our sins remitted? On the cross. During the Last Supper, the Lamb of God said he would take away the sins of the world when he died:

> This is my blood of the covenant, which is poured out for many for the forgiveness of sins. (Matthew 26:28)

30

Where was the Lord's blood poured out? At the cross. Where were all your sins forgiven? At the cross.

The thing about the *Thing*

Forgiveness in the new covenant is a noun not a verb; it's a gift not a work. It's something God gives, not something he does. (He's done it already.) This can be hard for us to understand because this is not how the world works. When you sin against someone, your relationship with that person comes under strain. There's this *Thing* that comes between the two of you. To be reconciled you need to deal with the *Thing*. Jesus said if you are bringing your gift to the altar and you remember your brother has some *Thing* against you, go and deal with that *Thing* (see Matthew 5:23). If your brother sins against you seven times in a day and seven times says, "I repent," forgive him. "Send that *Thing* away" (see Luke 17:4).

All this we know and understand. But here's the thing. God is not like you or me. He doesn't wait for you to act before he does his thing with your *Thing*. That *Thing* that was between you and him — your sin — he dealt with at the cross. Since God is not limited by time or space, he did not need to wait for you to start sinning before he forgave your sin. He has already forgiven you. He forgave you before you confessed, before you repented, before you were even born.

To forgive literally means to send forth or send away. Your sin hasn't merely been overlooked or covered up; it has been removed from you as far as the east is from the west. If you were to go looking for your sins, you wouldn't find them. They're gone.

> But now he has appeared once for all at the end of the ages to do away with sin by the sacrifice of himself. (Hebrews 9:26b)

At the cross, the sins of the world were sent away. This is why the risen Lord said we are to proclaim forgiveness as a done deal, rather than a favor to be earned.

No doubt the disciples were blown away when they heard this. First of all, there's Jesus standing among them when he's supposed to be dead. Second, he's preaching something that seems completely at odds with what he had said earlier in the Sermon on the Mount.

With the old covenant fulfilled and the new just getting underway, Jesus had to get his disciples up to speed quickly. He did this by opening their minds so they could understand scripture (Luke 24:44–45). He explained how the Law of Moses, the Prophets, and the Psalms all reached their fulfillment in him.

After their encounter with the risen Lord, the disciples began to see the old covenant with fresh eyes. Animal sacrifices and law-keeping, they now realized, could never take away sins. Those things only had value in that they pointed to Jesus. They also began to understand how the prophetic longings of Isaiah and Jeremiah, along with the radical, grace-based psalms of David, Asaph, and the Sons of Korah, heralded a day that had now dawned, namely, the new era of grace.[2]

On the cross the law was fulfilled, grace was revealed, and verbs became nouns. Forgiveness was no longer conditional on you doing A, B, and C. Forgiveness became a free gift paid for by the blood of the Lamb. How fitting, then, that the first people to hear this new message of unconditional forgiveness were the men of the Sanhedrin, the same men who had condemned Jesus to shed the very blood that paid for that forgiveness:

> God exalted him [Jesus] to his own right hand as Prince and Savior that he might *give* repentance and forgiveness of sins to Israel. (Act 5:31)

In other words, *Repentance is a gift! Forgiveness is a gift!*

When they heard these words, the old men of the Sanhedrin were furious. Unconditional forgiveness and risen Saviors had no place in their theology. Their religion was based on doing things for God not on God doing things for them. To the religious mind, grace is scandalous. Grace sounds like blasphemy.[3]

The old men had the apostles flogged and ordered them not to preach Jesus. Of course the apostles ignored this and years later, when Paul joined their ranks, he too began to preach the new message of unconditional forgiveness:

> I want you to know that through Jesus the forgiveness of sins is proclaimed to you. (Acts 13:38)

No hooks, no qualifications, no "turn from sin you brood of vipers." Just good news, delivered pure and straight.

What about John?

All this brings us to John who said:

> If we confess our sins, he is faithful and just to forgive us our sins and to cleanse us from all unrighteousness. (1 John 1:9, KJV)

This sounds like conditional forgiveness, like we have to review and take responsibility for our sins in order to be forgiven — and yet this comes after the cross. It's like a piece of the Old Testament accidentally got pasted into the New. What was John thinking? Was he napping when the risen Lord proclaimed forgiveness as an accomplished fact? How do we reconcile John with Jesus?

The usual way to read John is to attach a tiny price tag to the priceless gift of grace. "If you just do this small thing (acknowledge your sins), a good and gracious God will do this great thing (forgive your sins)." It sounds like a good deal but it's not. Indeed, given the phenomenal price Christ paid for your forgiveness, it's actually obscene. Allow me to illustrate.

If I gave you a mansion, with no strings attached, and you responded with, "Let me pay you with a piece of navel fluff — there, now we're square," I would be insulted. If you then went around telling others, "Give Paul your navel lint and he will give you mansions," I would do a facepalm. Then I would have to bolt my door to the hordes queuing outside with handfuls of fluff.

It is ridiculous to think you can pay God to forgive you. Yet many sincere believers are examining their navels for unconfessed sins because they think God is a sin collector who trades favors for sin. Hear that slapping sound? That's the sound of a hundred million angels doing facepalms!

The Creator is not some marionette you can manipulate through merit and money. He is the Almighty One, the Ancient of Days, who sits enthroned on high. In his wisdom and mercy he dealt with your sins once and for all at the cross.

John said, "He is faithful to forgive us our sins." From heaven's perspective, this seems an odd thing to say. God won't forgive you because he has *already* forgiven you. God doesn't judge the same sin twice, and at the cross he judged all sin. Consequently, he is no longer counting men's sins against them. Was John confused about grace? Not at all, for he goes on to explain that we were forgiven on account of his name (1 John 2:12). Forgiveness is based on his work not ours.

So why does John say God *will* forgive us our sins as though it was something he hadn't already done? Why does he sound like he is quoting the Old Testament? Because he *is* quoting the Old Testament. John is paraphrasing an Old Testament scripture to illuminate a New Testament concept. Look at the following two passages side by side and see if they resemble one another:

I said, "I will *confess* my transgressions to the Lord" — and you *forgave* the guilt of my sin. (Psalms 32:5b)	If we *confess* our sins, he is faithful and just to *forgive* us our sins and to cleanse us from all unrighteousness. (1 John 1:9, KJV)

New covenant confession

John is not preaching an old law (confess to be forgiven), he is using old and familiar language to describe something that would have been new and strange to his first-century readers. In this regard he is like Paul who quotes the same psalm in Romans 4:7-8. Paul quotes Psalm 32 to show we are blessed through faith and not works; John quotes Psalm 32 to show we won't be blessed except through faith. For this is what John means when he says we must confess. The Greek word for "confess" does not mean review your sins in the old covenant fashion, it means to agree with or say the same thing as another.[4] It means agreeing with what God has said, which is the essence of faith.

God has dealt with your sins whether you believe it or not but if you don't believe it then his forgiveness will be of no benefit to you. And you won't believe it if you are hearing sermons week after week about how sinful you are and how your sins are piling up to high heaven. If you are constantly being told to examine your heart for sin, bitterness, and unforgiveness, then you are going to have trouble trusting that you have been fully forgiven in Jesus' name. You're going to be susceptible to the sort of works-based, navel-gazing preaching that says you must acknowledge your faults and forgive to be forgiven.

From God's side, forgiveness is a done deal. There are no more sacrifices for sin. But from our side sin may be a serious problem indeed. So why do you need to receive the gift of forgiveness if you are already forgiven? For the same reason you need to receive the grace of God that has appeared to all men — it will change you. It will free you from guilt and condemnation and liberate you from captivity to sin.

An illustration may help: Let's say I do something truly wicked to you. Maybe I run over your cat or spread malicious lies about you. However, out of the goodness of your heart you decide to forgive me. *Such grace!* I don't deserve this. Your act of forgiveness is entirely based on your gracious character. Now if I continue to act wickedly toward you, then your forgiveness of me has had no effect in my life. From your side there may be no offense — all is forgiven — but from my side I am the same cat-killing, gossip-spreading sinner I always was.

Or perhaps I feel bad about what I did but I can't forgive myself for doing it. *I did such awful things!* What is the solution? It is not asking you to forgive me — you did that already. It is receiving the grace you have already put on the table. From your side I am forgiven, but as far as I'm concerned I either don't want your forgiveness or I don't know I have it. Your forgiveness leaves me unchanged because I have not received it.

Do you see? The grace of God has to be received to be effective in our lives. If you don't believe Jesus has saved you, then you're going to be short one Savior. If you don't believe the sins of the world were fully dealt with at the cross, then you're going to have trouble experiencing his forgiveness here and now.

The words of John—agree with God and you'll be forgiven—make perfect sense from our perspective. The moment you put your trust in Christ and his finished work, his forgiveness, which was there all the time, becomes real to you. In him we have the forgiveness of sins (Ephesians 1:7). You cannot be in Christ and be unforgiven any more than you can be in the ocean and be unwet.

How can we mess this up?

There are two ways to get this wrong: One, tell people that they must do something before God will forgive them—that's called law and it's a grace killer. Or two, tell sinners that because they are forgiven they are also saved—that's called universalism and it's a faith killer. Sadly, some have come racing out of one error only to dive headlong into the other. Let's be clear; forgiveness does not equal salvation. Although Christ carried the sins of the world on the cross, not everyone is saved.

Forgiveness is a manifestation of grace and grace has been given. Grace is on the table. But not everyone receives it. Salvation is not the absence of sin; salvation is the acceptance of God's grace.[5]

Some have asked me, "If we preach forgiveness as part of the finished work, isn't there a danger of promoting apathy and indifference among the lost?" There is, but there is a far greater danger if we don't preach forgiveness.

The opposite of forgiveness or remission is sin retention (John 20:23). Although the sins of the world were taken away at the cross, many people remain chained to sin through hurt and unforgiveness. They can't let go of the sins of those who have wounded them. Others can't let go of their own sins. They can't forgive themselves. They have camped at the places where they have blown it and the photo albums of their minds are full of past hurts. Those who have been wounded by sin may turn to religion for comfort, but religion without grace only makes things worse.

Just this morning I heard from a young man whose friend killed himself because he could not cope with the guilt religion had put on him. This is an awful tragedy but it should not surprise us. The Bible shows us again and again that any religion of rules ultimately ministers death to those who would live by them.[6] Grace-less religion kills people.

The only thing that can free people from the grip of sin is a revelation of God's grace. This is why it is essential that we heed Jesus and follow the apostles' example and proclaim the free gift of forgiveness. For some people it is literally a matter of life and death. They are dying for lack of forgiveness. The good news is that forgiveness is powerful. It heals, it restores, it liberates and brings reconciliation. Forgiveness saves lives.

The last thing this world needs is another guilt-shoveler behind a pulpit. What people desperately need to hear is the good news. They need to be told their sins have been forgiven and it is our responsibility to tell them. Indeed, this is the privilege of proclaiming the gospel.

The ministry of reconciliation is not telling people that a huffy God waits for them to sooth his offended ego with a bunch of repentance flowers and a box of confession chocolates. It is the thrill of proclaiming the glad, happy news that God loves them, his face is turned towards them, and he holds nothing against them.

Who are we?

There are two stumbling blocks in 1 John 1:9. The first stems from a misunderstanding of the word "confess" and the other stems from John's profligate use of the word "we." John says *we* need to confess and *we* need to be cleansed from all unrighteousness, but who are *we*? Us? Them? All of us? *Who?*

Read 1 John 1:9 in context and you will see that John is addressing people who do not have the truth in them, who are walking in darkness, and who need to be purified from all sin. Since a child of God is, by definition, someone who has the truth in them, walks in the light, and has been purified from all sin, John can only be referring to unbelievers. We can be doubly sure

John is not addressing believers in this passage because he says his motivation for writing is so "*you* may have fellowship with *us* and the Father." *You* are not *us*. *You* need to get connected to the life of God found in Jesus and shared by *us*, the body of Christ.[7]

But there's a problem with these particular unbelievers: They don't see their need for grace. They are of the opinion that they are without sin. In other words, they have a terminal case of self-righteousness and do not see themselves as sinners in need of a Savior. What John says to these people can best be understood if we first hear a little story.

Tough love for drunks and sinners

Brennan Manning tells a tale about a new patient at an alcoholic rehabilitation centre. The patient, Max, appeared to the group to be a healthy and respectable citizen. When grilled by the counselor over his drinking habits, Max described his behavior in a way that indicated he had no problem with alcohol. The counselor was not convinced. "You're a liar!" he shouted. "You drink like a pig." Max smiled, refusing to be drawn. He knew that his drinking was modest. He had nothing to be ashamed of.

The counselor picked up the phone and rang Max's bartender. It turns out Max was drinking considerably more than he let on. Max exploded with rage. He swore at the bartender and spat on the rug before regaining his composure. His outburst was justifiable, said Max. Even Jesus lost his temper.

The counselor pressed further. "Have you ever been unkind to your kids?" Max did remember some unpleasantness involving his nine-year-old daughter but he couldn't recall the details. The counselor rang Max's wife and got the whole story.

Max had taken his little girl shopping for a Christmas present and on the way home he had stopped at a tavern for a drink. He locked his daughter in the car promising her he would be right out. It was an extremely cold day so he left the motor running. At midnight Max staggered out, drunk. The motor had stopped running and the car windows had frozen shut. His daughter was so badly frostbitten the doctors had to amputate two of her fingers. They said she would be deaf for the rest of her life.

2. Forgiven

Confronted by the horror of his sin, Max's mask of self-made respectability shattered and he collapsed on the floor sobbing hysterically. The counselor put his boot into Max's side and rolled him onto his back. "You are unspeakable slime!" the counselor roared. "Get out before I throw up. I am not running a rehab for liars!"[8]

Manning's point is that tough love is essential when you're dealing with lying alcoholics. "In order to free the captive, one must name the captivity." Before he can be helped, Max has to recognize his need for help.

The same is true of sinners. If you don't think sin is a serious business, then you won't value the grace of God. You will be blasé about his forgiveness, and you will treat grace as a license to sin.

It's not hard to find respectable sinners in church. They come in, like Max, with their masks of pretentious piety and put on a good show. They lead home groups and volunteer for the working bee. They tell a good story and make a good impression. But inside they are full of dead men's bones.

Counselor John was not fooled by outward appearances. Knowing his letter would be widely read, he speaks plainly to all the Maxes of the world:

If we claim that we experience a shared life with him and continue to stumble around in the dark, we're obviously lying through our teeth ... If we claim that we're free of sin, we're only fooling ourselves. (1 John 1:6,8, The Message)

In other words, "You sinners who think you're hot stuff, who don't believe you're sinners in need of saving, you are unspeakable slime! Get out before I throw up. I am not running a church for liars!"[9]

To reiterate, John is not speaking to the children of God. His tone completely changes when he addresses "my little children" at the beginning of the next chapter. In this passage John is confronting religious wingnuts who have infiltrated the church with grace-less and cross-less heresies. What message does John have for these frauds and phonies?

> Stop calling God a liar and agree with him — *confess!* — that you are a sinner in need of forgiveness. Do that and God will be faithful and just to forgive not just the sins you did today, but the sins you did yesterday and the sins you are going to do tomorrow. Indeed, he will cleanse you from all unrighteousness.

How can John be so sure about this? Because in a manner of speaking, God has already done it.

The cure for condemnation

Maybe you are struggling with sin and carrying truckloads of guilt. Perhaps you wear shame like a cloak. The solution to your problem is standing on a hill 2,000 years in the past. On the cross Jesus became the propitiation for the sins of the whole world (1 John 2:2). Propitiation is a big word but it simply means Jesus turned God's wrath away from the sin that was in you and me by taking our sin to the cross.

Sin is like a lightning rod; it attracts wrath. Throughout Old Testament history flashes of judgment would occasionally vaporize some poor soul or race whose sin grew too big to be ignored. But on the cross Jesus took the sin of the world and obliterated it in one mighty blast of judgment. He paid the ultimate price so that we could live totally forgiven and free.

Your sins have been done away with. They have been blotted out, abolished, canceled, and dismissed. They have been fried as if by lightning. This is supposed to make you happy:

> Happy are those whose wrongs are forgiven, whose sins are pardoned! Happy is the person whose sins the Lord will not keep account of! (Romans 4:7–8, GNB)

Yet many are not happy. They are racked with guilt, unable to forgive themselves or others because they have not seen the lightning rod of the cross. They have not heard the stunning news that Jesus' sacrifice is the once and final solution for their sin. Instead they have been led to believe that God is angry with them, that he is keeping accounts, and building a case against them. They have been sold a counterfeit brand of forgiveness that comes straight from Sinai instead of the real forgiveness that comes from Calvary.

If God's love is unconditional, then his forgiveness must be unconditional too. And it is! His forgiveness is not doled out in proportion to our acts of repentance or confession. It is lavished upon us according to the riches of his grace (Ephesians 1:7). You only need to look at Jesus to know this is true.

During his time on earth, Jesus went around forgiving people who neither confessed nor repented, and while he hung on the cross he forgave those who put him there. The Son of God did all this to give us a picture of what true forgiveness looks like; it looks like love.

You need to treat God's forgiveness the same way you treat his love—as a gift received by faith from start to finish. You don't need to beat yourself up to get it; you just need to look to the cross and say, "Thank you, Jesus."

"But won't I lose his forgiveness if I continue to sin? What about the sin I did just this morning?" Like all your sins this one was dealt with at the cross. It was not recorded as a black mark next to your name because God is not in the business of imputing sin.[10] It is human nature to keep score but it is not God's nature. God is love and love keeps no record of wrongs. If you were to ask him about this morning's sin, he would say, "What sin? I have no record of that sin. Stop looking for it and look to Jesus."

If you are battling with guilt and condemnation, heed the words of Jesus and proclaim his forgiveness over yourself. Look at yourself in the mirror and confess what the Bible says is true about you:

I have been redeemed by the blood of the Lamb. I have been saved from sin and I know I am. All my sins are taken away. Praise the Lord![11]

Then take those guilty and condemning thoughts and make them bow to the One who carried your sins away and who bled to purchase your eternal forgiveness.

The gospel of forgiveness

The words of Jesus and John have been taken out of context, turned upside down, and used to sow confusion and uncertainty among many. In the fruitless pursuit of a free gift we have wasted time trying to manage each other's sin through the power of the flesh. Instead of going out into the highways and byways with the good news of grace, we have cloistered ourselves away to examine our hearts and stare at our navels. From the devil's point of view, it has been a phenomenally successful distraction.

Running after forgiveness is like shopping for air. Air is free! God has already given us all the air we will ever need. You just need to open your mouth and breathe it in. It's the same with his forgiveness. Forgiveness is not something to pursue, it is something to possess and in Christ we have it.

The gospel is not an invitation to engage in soul-searching and fault-finding. The gospel is the emphatic declaration that you have been completely and eternally forgiven through the blood of the Lamb.

It is by grace you have been saved. (Ephesians 2:5)

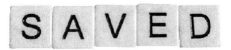

The word "saved" has a strange effect on people. Some get quite upset by it. I have had churchgoers rebuke me because I happened to mention that some are saved while others are unsaved. Apparently that's not a politically correct thing to say. Others find the word a bit meaningless believing "we were all saved" or "none of us is yet saved" or "we are saved and being saved at the same time." Still others treat the word as an invitation to hunker down in the proverbial lifeboat and do nothing while the rest of the world goes to hell in a handbasket. "Thank God I'm saved. Now I'm just going to sit tight 'til Jesus returns."

The gospel of salvation is the gospel every Christian thinks they know. "Oh yes, once I was lost, now I am saved." Salvation, however you define it, is also the area where most believers are likely to stand on grace. "I am saved by grace alone. My works don't come into it." But while these broad strokes paint a fair picture, the devil lurks in the details.

Let's start with a straightforward question: Are you saved?

In this age of political correctness, some find this question offensive for it leads to divisions between the right sort of people (the saved) and the wrong (the unsaved). Certainly, it is ungracious to draw lines and nobody likes to be told they are on the wrong side or, worse, that they are the wrong sort of person. But the sad fact is the world is a hospice, a home for the terminally ill. It makes no difference how good or moral you are, the end result is the same for everyone. All fall short of God's glory, and the wages of our sin is death.[1] In a manner of speaking, we are all the wrong sort of person. But the good news declares it doesn't have to be this way. Sin no longer has the last word on our situation.

The gospel is the happy and joyful announcement that a Savior works in the hospice giving eternal life to the terminally ill. He has a 100 percent success rate, and he will gladly treat anyone who wants to be treated. What's the catch? There is no catch. The treatment is completely free; it won't cost you a penny.[2] And the best part is this Savior is so good at what he does, he can revive the worst, the sickest, and most hopeless case in the ward. No one is beyond his skill.

> So do not be ashamed to testify about our Lord, or ashamed of me his prisoner. But join with me in suffering for the gospel, by the power of God, who has saved us ... (2 Timothy 1:8-9)

There has always been opposition to the gospel of salvation but there is no shame in saving lives. Paul said to Timothy, "He has saved us." In other words, we're okay but they're not okay. They are not saved. They haven't heard. They need to hear. So join with me, Timothy, and don't ever be ashamed of telling people the good news of Dr. Jesus.

The gospel that saves

Paul was a highly educated man used to moving in elevated circles. But when he began preaching the gospel of salvation, his message came across as offensive to Jews and foolishness to Gentiles. It was just too simple for them to see it. They couldn't wrap their minds around the fact that a man from heaven had died and risen again to save us from the curse of sin and death. Yet despite the violent opposition he sometimes faced, Paul was resolute. He never changed his tune. He stuck with the gospel because it is the only message that can save the dying.

> I am not ashamed of the gospel, because it is the power of God for the salvation of everyone who believes: first for the Jew, then for the Gentile. (Romans 1:16)

Paul insisted there was only one gospel that saved people and that was his gospel. "By *this* gospel you are saved" (1 Corinthians 15:2). Other gospels, he said, were perversions. They weren't good news at all. Those who preached them could go to hell because that's where their false gospels would take them.[3] Paul didn't really want to condemn anyone to hell, and he had no interest in dividing people into groups. "In Christ, there is neither Jew nor Greek, male nor female" (see Galatians 3:28). But he understood that people divide themselves by their response to truth.

Truth is divisive by nature. Jesus, who is Truth personified, said he came to turn "a man against his father, a daughter against her mother" such that "a man's enemies will be members of his own household" (Matthew 10:35-36). It's not that Jesus came to split families; he came to save them. But not everyone wants to be saved. Sometimes fathers and sons want different things. The gospel is the power of God for the salvation of everyone who believes, but not everyone believes. Strange as it may seem, not everyone trusts the Doctor with the 100 percent record:

Most assuredly, I say to you, he who believes in me has everlasting life. (John 6:47, NKJV)

Are you saved? Well that depends on your response to the Savior. That depends on whether you trust in his grace.

For it is by grace you have been saved, through faith — and this not from yourselves, it is the gift of God. (Ephesians 2:8)

The grace of God is worthless if you don't believe in it (Hebrews 4:2). Grace can save anyone but grace scorned saves no one. Dr. Jesus does not force salvation on the unwilling. As with any gift you have to want it to receive it.

So faith is essential but don't overcook it. Christians tend to fret that they don't have enough faith as though faith was something you have to manufacture. Not so. Jesus is the fountainhead of faith. It is seeing and hearing about Jesus — who he is and what he has done—that stirs us to believe (Romans 10:17). It is a revelation of God's unconditional love that moves us to trust him.

Faith is not us making things happen. Neither does faith compel God to act as though he were a genie in a bottle. What is faith? Faith is simply a positive response to something God has said or done. And what has God done? He has raised Jesus from the dead proving that any claims held on our lives by sin have been fully satisfied and that Jesus really is the firstfruits of new life.

The resurrection is the key to all of this. The resurrection is proof that Jesus is who he says he is and that he can do what he says he can. The resurrection demonstrates that the Savior has broken the power of death and is able to give new life to all who would have it. A dead Savior saves no one.

Faith is simply trusting in Jesus. If you do not believe Jesus is the risen Lord, then the fact of his risenness will do you no good. How could it?

Is everyone saved?

It is popular these days to teach that the whole world was saved at the cross, that Jesus died not as humanity's representative but as humanity itself. Those who preach this message typically ask, "Jesus came to save the world—did he fail?"

I am certain Jesus accomplished all he came to do, and yet not everyone is saved. If they were, why would the apostles risk life and limb preaching that *we must be saved*? Why would they write letters telling us that God *wants us to be saved* and that he commands people everywhere to repent and believe in the name of his Son in order *to be saved*? For that matter, why would the risen Lord commission us to preach the good news to all creation so that whoever believes *might be saved*?[4]

The grace of God that brings salvation has appeared to all men (Titus 2:11), but not all receive it. Consequently, not all are saved. Jesus said: "I am the door. If anyone enters by me, he will be saved ... (John 10:9, NKJV). Trusting in the Savior is the requirement for salvation (Acts 16:31). There is nothing wrong with telling believers they are saved and there is nothing wrong with telling unbelievers they can be. Believers need the assurance, and unbelievers need to hear the good news.

When I was a young Christian, I had no assurance of my salvation. Full of doubt and insecurity I gave my life to Jesus repeatedly over a period of about three years. The problem was I thought my salvation was based on what I did. This is an unbearable load. *What if I did it wrong? There is an awful lot riding on that one prayer – how can I be sure I got it right? I can't. I'd better do it again.* What I needed was someone to tell me the good news of *his* salvation: "Whosoever calls on the name of the Lord will be saved."[5] If you have called, then you are saved. Believe it. Rest in it.

Fallen from grace

Most Christians have a decent enough grasp of the gospel of salvation. They've heard enough about grace to know they need it to be saved. But while they may see Jesus in the big picture of salvation, they often miss the devil in the details.

Those details usually emerge from the mouths of evangelists who try to sell the extravagant gift of grace for a small price: "Just turn from your wicked ways ... just confess your sins ... just do this one small thing for Jesus." At first it all seems so reasonable. Who wouldn't want to turn or confess or turn cartwheels through daisy fields when seized by the power of a great affection? Don't misunderstand me; I am not against any of these things. But saying you must do them in order to be saved is the thin edge of a diabolical wedge. Just look at what happens next.

The one who responds to the evangelist's invitation is presented with a slightly longer list of deeds. "Now that you're a Christian you have to read your Bible and pray every day, join a church, and go tell others about Jesus." Keen to please the Lord who saved him, the new believer reads his Bible and what does he find? More things to do; more rules to keep. He attends the new members' meeting at his new church and what does he get? Still more rules and more expectations.

Guess what, kid, it never ends.

It's not long before the small list becomes a big list and suddenly following Jesus is sheer hard work. The more he learns about the Christian life, the more he finds he must do:

Here are three keys to resisting temptation, five steps to overcoming sin, and eight more to walking in victory. Don't forget to pursue the spiritual disciplines, attend the pre-dawn prayer meeting and the midnight mass. Please support these eighteen worthwhile causes, get behind this new program, and, while you're at it, how about helping out with the youth group on Fridays and Sundays? On Saturday we expect you to lend a hand with the church clean-up and we hope you will spend your vacation time building our new prayer chapel.

The new believer was told Jesus would set him free but he doesn't feel free at all. He feels like a worker ant toiling for the good of the colony.

To keep the worker ant motivated, the higher-ups will provide a steady stream of rousing pep talks: "I would rather serve in the courts of the Lord than dwell in the tents of the wicked." For extra productivity they may also crack the whip of guilt: "Look how much Jesus has done for you. What will you do for him?" To advance whatever cause they have bought into they will manipulate emotions, pretend to speak for God, and shame those who fail to perform.

And when the worker ant eventually breaks under the ungodly weight of works, they will shoot him and toss his broken corpse outside the anthill. "If you won't work, you won't eat." So grace dies and the devil wins.

Swallow the lie that says you must prove your salvation through works—that faith without self-effort is dead—and you will have fallen from grace as hard as any Galatian. Fallen from grace does not mean fallen into sin or fallen out of the kingdom.[6] Fallen from grace means you are trying instead of trusting. Instead of resting in his work, you are trying to score points with yours. Whether you are working towards justification, sanctification, or whatever, it just won't work. Grace cannot be earned. God does not keep score.

Continuing in faith

The gospel of your salvation was underwritten by the most precious commodity in the universe; the blood of the Lamb. Jesus paid a high price for your redemption. The problem with asking you to do anything for Jesus is that it can leave you trusting in what you have done instead of resting in what he has done. "I turned from sin, therefore I must be saved. I avoid wickedness, and do good works, therefore I must be *really* saved." No, no, no! That's old covenant thinking. It's mixing faith in what he's done with faith in what you've done. It is setting aside grace. Jesus didn't do most of it; he did all of it. Trust him alone.

> He saved us, not because of righteous things we had done,
> but because of his mercy. (Titus 3:5a)

Jesus is the author *and* the finisher. He doesn't just get you started; he completes what he began. This is why old Christians need the gospel just as much as young sinners. Grace is for everyone. Grace saves you at the beginning and it keeps you through to the end. This was something the Colossian Christians needed to be reminded of.

> So then, just as you received Christ Jesus as Lord, continue to live in him, rooted and built up in him, strengthened in the faith as you were taught, and overflowing with thankfulness. (Colossians 2:6–7)

How did you receive Jesus? By faith. How should you continue to live in him? By faith. It's faith in his all-sufficient grace from first to last.

> But now he has reconciled you by Christ's physical body through death to present you holy in his sight, without blemish and free from accusation — if you continue in your

faith, established and firm, not moved from the hope held out in the gospel. (Colossians 1:22–23a)

This sounds like a conditional statement, as though you are saved for as long as "you continue in your faith." It sounds like you can lose your salvation. As we will see in the next chapter, that is simply not possible. When you were born again you became something new; you were put into Christ. If you are faithless, he remains faithful for he cannot disown himself (2 Timothy 2:13). Once you have been born you cannot be unborn.

Here in Colossians Paul is talking about falling from grace and coming back under the influence of carnal religion, or what he calls "hollow and deceptive philosophy, which depends on human tradition and the basic principles of this world rather than on Christ" (Colossians 2:8). He is talking about any teaching that promotes trust in self rather than Christ. The point is not that God changes his mind but that we can change ours. We can go from trusting to trying, from resting to striving. When that happens God remains as gracious as ever, but we no longer experience his grace. We become distracted and, as far as we are concerned, cut off from grace. We begin to doubt our identity and we stop acting like who we really are.

How do we avoid falling from grace? How do we continue in the faith? We have to hold fast to the "hope held out in the gospel." We need to take care that we are not seduced by the false hopes offered by grace-less religion.

Religion will tell you that you are incomplete and in lack and that you have to work to get what you don't have. But the gospel Paul preached declares "you have been given fullness in Christ" (Colossians 2:10). In him you don't lack a thing. Religion says God may forgive your sins if you play your cards right and behave, but the gospel declares "he forgave us all our sins" already (Colossians 2:13). Religion says God relates to us through grace when we're good and through the law when we sin: But the gospel says he canceled and nailed to the cross "the written code, with its regulations, that was against us and that stood opposed to us" (Colossians 2:14). God doesn't relate to us on the basis of grace some of the time but all of the time. He never changes.

The gospel of heaven is infinitely better than the religion of earth. Manmade religion would have you trust in yourself dooming you to certain failure. But the good news of grace inspires trust in the Lord who has already won and who therefore can never fail. Why is it that those who see this are overflowing with thankfulness? It's not because we have learned to be grateful for the little things like the grass and sunshine. It is because Jesus is supremely good at saving us:

> Therefore he [Jesus] is able also to save to the uttermost (completely, perfectly, finally, and for all time and eternity) those who come to God through him, since he is always living to make petition to God and intercede with him and intervene for them. (Hebrews 7:25, AMP)

Jesus is our Great Redeemer and our only Savior. He is the One who stills the storms and calls us to dance with him upon the waves.

And this brings us, finally, to the lifeboats.

Scuttle the lifeboats

The lifeboat gospel is the idea that salvation is all about avoiding hell and gaining heaven. The problem with this gospel is that it has sidelined entire generations of believers by telling them the earth is nothing more than a waiting room for eternity.

Afraid of being left behind, Christians with a lifeboat mentality have opted out of the game. They want nothing to do with this filthy world lest they end up entangled in it. "Forget the arts, forget politics, forget science. This world is destined for the fire anyway, so why bother."

Lifeboat Christians are hands-off Christians. Yet their passivity, which is really unbelief, means they regularly get steamrolled by the circumstances of life. When this happens it only confirms their belief that "the ship is sinking — you'd best get off."[7]

Selling a gospel of salvation-*later* robs people of the benefits of salvation-*now*. The word most commonly translated as "save" in the Bible, *sozo*, literally means to deliver, protect, heal, preserve,

51

and make whole.[8] It covers not only salvation in eternity, but healing, deliverance, and prosperity today.

When God created the earth, everything was good. There was no sickness, oppression, or poverty. All that bad stuff came later as a result of sin. If the Savior's sacrifice is the once-and-for-all-time cure for sin, surely his salvation is the cure for all the effects of sin, otherwise his work remains unfinished.

During his time on earth, Jesus revealed the gospel of salvation through signs and wonders. When he healed the sick, he *sozo*-ed them; he made them whole. To be saved literally means to be made whole. Jesus said those who followed him would do what he did. He said this not to put pressure on you — we're under grace, remember — but to call you and me to the abundant life that is ours by right. We who are saved for eternity have been left in the hospice to release his salvation power to the sick and dying. Salvation is not for the distant hereafter; salvation is for now. Today is the day of salvation; now is the time of God's favor.

> Therefore, my dear friends, as you have always obeyed — not only in my presence, but now much more in my absence — continue to work out your salvation with fear and trembling, for it is God who works in you to will and to act according to his good purpose. (Philippians 2:12–13)

When you first put your faith in Jesus, you crossed over from death to life. Eternal life is already yours and you are one with the Lord. But in this life we face many challenges. Working out your salvation means receiving, by faith, the grace you need to get through today. God has already given you the gift of salvation — it is within you — now work it out. Take that gift and use it to bring change to your circumstances. Instead of living in reaction to doctor's reports, bills, and problems at work, learn to live in reaction to what God has said and done. This is what it means to walk in the spirit. It's walking by faith rather than sight. It is trusting in his all-sufficient grace in your hour of need.

Fear and trembling

Why does Paul encourage us to work out our salvation with fear and trembling? Because faith is risky. Faith often runs contrary to what our eyes and ears are telling us, and this is why we tremble. If the doctor says you have a week to live, your emotions will react with fear and trembling. You will have to strive to enter his rest in the midst of your trouble. But Paul says do it anyway — fix your eyes on Jesus despite the fear — "for it is God who works in you."

Paul knew something about this for he went to Corinth "in weakness and fear and with much trembling" (1 Corinthians 2:3). Paul didn't know what was going to happen in that pagan city but he went anyway, despite his fear, because it was his passion to bring the light of the gospel to the Gentiles. And as he began to preach Jesus Christ and him crucified, the Holy Spirit showed up with a demonstration of supernatural power (see 1 Corinthians 2:1–5). This is what it means to co-labor with the Lord. We work out or express what God has put within us, and he confirms his word through signs and wonders.

Why are fear and trembling involved? Because learning to walk in the new way of the spirit can be scary. The first time you offer to pray for a sick person can be frightening. "What if they don't get healed?" *What if they do!* Since they are already sick, what have you got to lose? The first time you pray or write or speak or stand on your head in the name of Jesus is going to be the hardest. But you will never experience of the thrill of co-laboring with Christ if you put fear ahead of faith.[9]

The woman who had been bleeding for twelve years risked much by reaching out to Jesus. As one who was ceremonially unclean, she was supposed to keep her distance from other people. Being pushy in a crowd was illegal and indecent. Yet with fear and trembling she risked everything because she wanted healing and she knew where to get it. When she touched the hem of the Savior's garment he turned to her and said, "Have courage, your faith has made you whole."[10] Technically, she wasn't healed by her faith but by the grace of God. But since grace only comes to us through faith, Jesus said what he said. We access his reservoirs of grace through faith.

I have been in meetings where faith sizzled in the air like electricity and hundreds were healed. I've also been in situations where I was the only one praying in a room full of skeptics. Can you guess which setting involved more fear and trembling on my part?

Now we begin to understand why Paul encouraged the Philippians to go for it "all the more in my absence." I'm sure they had a fine old time when the mighty Paul was in town. How could you *not* get healed when the man with the miraculous hanky was around (see Acts 19:11–12)? But Paul is not the magic man and we should be able to do this without him. That's why Paul tells them and us, "Learn to do this on your own. You can! You don't need me or some anointed guy with flashy white teeth and a suit. It's your faith in his grace that releases salvation power. It is God who works in you."

And again, lest we get hung up on the faith side of the equation, Paul reminds us two verses earlier that it's not about him or us or the anointed guy in the suit but Jesus under whose name "every knee should bow, in heaven and on earth and under the earth" (Philippians 2:10).

Salvation, whether we're talking about healing, deliverance, or financial breakthrough, is what happens when our daily needs are made to bow to name of the Savior Jesus.

The gospel of salvation

The gospel of salvation is good news for a race cursed by sin, for it reveals the power of God for healing, deliverance, and eternal life. As a believer, your future is secure in him. Your spirit is one with the Lord, inseparably linked, and eternally saved. But our bodies and minds still suffer the slings and arrows of outrageous fortune, and for the time being the world remains under the influence of the evil one (1 John 5:19). Life can be hard. But life does not have the last word for those who choose to walk in the spirit. Bad news may come, but the good news is that we are more than conquerors through him who loved us.

The gospel is not merely a promise of a ticket to heaven and a distant salvation. The gospel is the power of God to bless you with his saving and abundant life here and now. That life is found in knowing him and trusting him in the midst of your circumstances. The good news of his salvation declares that it is not his will for you to be sick or poor. If you are, don't blame God. Jesus said it's the thief who comes to rob and destroy (John 10:10). God is not making you sick or broke to teach you character. His will is for you to prosper in all things, even as your soul prospers (3 John 1:2).

The gospel of salvation declares that on the cross the Savior made full provision for your complete salvation. In him you have been blessed with every spiritual blessing. You don't have to ask for whatever it is you need; in him you've already got it. You just need to work it out in your life through faith.

When you understand the good news of his salvation it will change the way you pray. Instead of asking God to do what he has already done, you will move in the power and authority he has given you and shamelessly proclaim the name of King Jesus over your circumstances. Instead of talking to God about your problems, you'll talk to your problems about your God.

As you grow in the confidence that he who saves you also keeps you, you will leave the dubious comfort of the lifeboat and return to the *Titanic* where you will bring the good news of salvation to others. You will lay hands on the sick and they will be healed. You will proclaim freedom to the captives and they will be freed. You will find that supernatural signs and wonders follow this good news wherever it goes.

But God has brought you into union with Christ Jesus ...
(1 Corinthians 1:30, GNB)

U N I O N

Camilla and I got married at four o'clock in the afternoon. Our wedding banquet kicked off at six o'clock. The two hours between the "I do" and "Let's party!" were two of the sweetest, yet most surreal, hours of my life. During the photo taking and guest-greeting I kept looking at this beautiful woman next to me in amazement. *This lady is my wife. I have a wife? I didn't have a wife this morning. How did this happen? All I said was 'I do.'*

I now know why they have parties at weddings. It's to give the startled bride and groom a chance to process the shock and the wonder of what just happened. *This is for real. I thought I was dreaming but look at all these smiling people. They seem pretty convinced we're married so we must be married.*

Jesus once spoke of the joy that erupts in heaven when a sinner repents and comes to believe in the good news. We might imagine they have something like a birthday party to celebrate the new birth, but in reality it's the rejoicing that accompanies a wedding. It's a celebration of a new life wedded in union with Christ.

Many of us are looking forward to the wedding banquet yet to come, but Jesus is returning for his bride, not his fiancée. You are already married to him. Your union with Christ is not a future event but a present reality that began the moment you first said "Yes" to Jesus. You are now living in the two hours between the "I do" and "Let's party!" It's sweet, a bit surreal, but you are most definitely wed.

Married to Jesus

Jesus said, "I am the vine, you are the branches," and from that most wonderful affirmation of our union, confused preachers have drawn terrifying lessons about being cut off and thrown into the fire. Whoa. Slow down. That's like fretting about divorce in the middle of your honeymoon. Relax. Jesus doesn't believe in divorce. In fact he hates it. You're stuck with him for good. What God has joined together, let no man separate.[1]

Look at those words again: "I am the vine, you are the branches" (John 15:5). Your union with Christ is not a far-off event but an accomplished fact. You are already in Christ. Since there is no part of the branch that is not also part of the vine, anyone who touches you touches Jesus. When you place your hands on the sick, you are placing his hands on the sick. When you open your mouth to speak the good news, you are speaking his words with his mouth.

I have been married for some time so I don't find this strange at all. I am accustomed to thinking in terms of a one-flesh team. I remind Camilla about this every time the parent-teacher interviews come up at school. "But honey, we don't need to *both* go, for if *you* are there then *we* are there. We're a one-flesh team." And she usually responds by giving me a sideways glance.

I jest to make an important point. Our one-flesh union is an earthly picture of the spiritual union all believers have with Jesus:

On that day you will realize that I am in my Father, and you are in me, and I am in you. (John 14:20)

He is in you and you are in him. Wherever you go, he goes. When you go to the parent-teacher interview, the Lord of the Universe goes with you.

"Wait a second, Paul. How can Jesus be *here* with us if he's up *there* with the Father?" That's a good question. How can Jesus be in two places at once? How can he be present within every believer at the same time?

Before Jesus returned to heaven, he said to the disciples: "It is for your good that I go away" (John 16:7). Jesus said the Comforter would come after he left and we would be better off with him than we were with Jesus being physically present. He was saying, "I have been *with* you, and that has been good, but soon I will be *in* you, and that will be even better."

The Holy Spirit is the answer to the question, "How can Jesus leave us and be with us at the same time?" Since the Holy Spirit is the Spirit of Christ, to be filled with the Spirit is to be filled with Jesus. And since he who has the Son also has the Father, to be filled with Jesus is to be filled with the Father as well. He who has the Spirit also has the Son and the Father. They are an inseparable team.[2]

Right after promising the Holy Spirit, Jesus said, "I will not leave you as orphans." An orphan is a fatherless child. Jesus was saying you won't be that person. "My Father and I will come to you and make our home with you" (see John 14:23). You have not been filled with one-third of God but all of him; Father, Son, and Spirit.

For better or worse

Some people understand this but only half way. "Sure, God is with us, but sometimes he isn't. He comes and he goes." It's true that in the Old Testament the Holy Spirit came upon certain people at certain times, but that was then and this is now. Jesus said the Holy Spirit abides with us and makes his home with us (John 14:16-17). By home he means *home*. You are not a motel room for the Lord. You are a walking, talking, living, breathing temple of the Holy Spirit. He is not going anywhere.

"Are you saying that the Holy Spirit is with me even when I sin?" Yes! Christ's love for you and his union with you is stronger than any sin.

Under the old covenant, sinning was your fast track to disunion. If you sinned you risked being cut off from the people of God. Jesus said if your hand or eye causes you to sin, get rid of it (Matthew 5:29-30). Why did Jesus preach self-amputation to those born under the law? Because under that covenant it made awful sense to talk about removing those parts of the body that might contaminate the whole. Thank the Lord the old covenant is gone.

We are not under law but grace, and this is good news for the members of the body of Christ.

When we sin, Jesus does not cut us off; we remain members of his body. This totally changes the way we look at sin.

> Shall I then take the members of Christ and unite them with a prostitute? Never! (1 Corinthians 6:15b)

Under the old covenant we were restrained from sin through mortal terror but in the new we are restrained by love. Look again at Paul's warning about prostitutes. Behind the warning—don't do it—there is a surprising and reassuring affirmation of union. Paul is saying it is possible, though not advisable, to unite the members of Christ's body with prostitutes. Do you see it? Earthly marriages may break and fail, but your union with Christ is unbreakable. Sin cannot break it. Addiction cannot break it. The stupidest decisions you might ever make cannot break it.

This should not be taken as a challenge to see what you can get away with but as a stunning declaration of Christ's absolute commitment to love you and stick with you *no matter what*. This is what changes us—not the weak influence of the rule (there is no rule; all things are lawful) but the relentless and determined passion of his love.

The love of God is the greatest force in the universe. Sin wilts before it. When you encounter the undaunted and unending love of Christ, it changes you. You no longer want to sin. The passing pleasures of this world lose their appeal because you have found a love that is truer and better by far.

No more lonely love songs

Union with Christ is the number one reason why we have it better than those who lived before the cross. Back then they wrote love songs about yearning and absence. "I looked for the one my heart loves but I could not find him." "I opened to my beloved, but my beloved was gone." "As the deer pants for the water, so my soul pants for you, O God."[3] It breaks my heart to hear Christians singing songs of longing and calling it worship. I imagine it breaks

Jesus' heart too. Where are you Lord? *I am right here. I am in you and you are in me.* Where did you go? *I didn't go anywhere. I promised I would never leave you.*

Here's another timeless classic from the album, *Love Songs of the Old Covenant*:

> One thing I ask of the Lord, this is what I seek: that I may dwell in the house of the Lord all the days of my life. (Psalms 27:4a)

That you *may* dwell in the house of the Lord? You *are* the house of the Lord. You can dwell in the house of the Lord as long as you like. In fact, it's going to be quite impossible for you to dwell anywhere else.

To see how well you grasp this, ask yourself a simple question: Where is God? When you think of God being some *place*, where is that place? Is he up there or over there or who knows where? Well I suppose God can be anywhere and everywhere, but the good news declares he is in you and you are in him. Any concept of separating distance is totally demolished by this revelation. He is not far away and he is not hiding behind a cloud. How can we be sure? Because Jesus said so. "Surely I am with you always" (Matthew 28:20).

Intimacy is not something we ever need long for. (He is already with us.) We don't have to beg God to rend the heavens and come down. (He already did.) And we never have to fear that he might abandon us as orphans. (He promised he wouldn't.) The good news declares that now and forever more, you are in perfect union with the Lord.

Sing to the Lord a new song

The Holy Spirit is the key to understanding the mystery of our union. Tragically, the Holy Spirit has been painted as the sheriff of heaven when in truth he is the one pouring out the love of God into your heart.

Look back at the movie of your life with Jesus and you will find the Holy Spirit's directing influence behind every scene. Who do you think was the One who first revealed Jesus to you? Who opened your heart to believe and your mouth to confess that Jesus is Lord? The Holy Spirit is the reason you are reading this, and he is the one encouraging you to believe all this good stuff I'm telling you about Jesus. If you have been in the habit of singing old love songs of longing and loneliness, he will give you new songs of intimacy and fulfillment. In short, the Holy Spirit is the best friend you ever had.

> Or don't you know that all of us who were baptized into Christ Jesus were baptized into his death? (Romans 6:3)

I used to think this was a verse about water baptism but it's not. This verse is describing the real baptism of which water baptism is but a reenactment. You have been baptized into Jesus Christ.

To baptize means to dip in the sense of dipping cloth into dye. White cloth goes in; purple cloth comes out. Something like that happened to you when you were dipped into Christ by the Holy Spirit. You went in looking like Adam; you came out looking like Jesus. Before you were baptized you were alienated from the life of God; afterwards you were connected to the life-giving vine. How did this happen? I don't know. Ask the Holy Spirit. He's the one who did it.[4] You don't need to have it all figured out to benefit from it. You just need to say, "Thank you, Holy Spirit."

> For if we have been planted together in the likeness of his death, we shall be also in the likeness of his resurrection. (Romans 6:5, KJV)

There is a word in this verse that appears nowhere else in the Bible. It is a word that excites theologians into hand-waving bursts of hyper-ventilated hermeneutics. It is the word *sumphutos* which is here translated as "planted together." This is just about the strongest word for union you could possibly think of. It means being "born together with" or "of joint origin." The closest English word is *connate* which means individual parts that are united to form a single whole.[5] The best illustration of connate union is the one Jesus gave us—a vine and a branch, two parts that combine to make an indivisible whole. Vines and branches cannot be understood in isolation. A vine that has no branches is not much of a vine, and a branch that is not part of a vine is not a branch. It's just a stick.

What does this connate union mean for us? It means our lives cannot be understood in isolation from Jesus. Apart from him we can do nothing. We can't bear fruit, we can't grow, and we can't live. This has been humanity's experience from the Year Dot.

When our first father and mother walked out on God they automatically cut themselves and their unborn descendants off from the tree of life. They severed the tie that sustained us and humanity became the broken branch that withered and died. But through his death and resurrection, Jesus made a way for us to be raised from the dead to new life. That life flows as the natural result of being connected in vital union with the Living Vine.

The fruits of union

The good news is we don't need to do a thing to make this new life happen, we just need to receive it. To partake in his divine nature requires only that we live in the union that is already ours.

You may say, "But I don't feel it. I don't feel connected." Don't put your faith in feelings. Believe the One who declares, "You are a branch." His eternal word is truer than your momentary feelings. "But I'm struggling to produce fruit." Stop struggling. It's not your job to produce fruit but to bear the fruit that he produces in you.

He is the vine. Quit trying to be a little vine of your own. Jesus does it all. Our part is to trust him and depend on him for everything. The fact is you are in union, so live in union. Act married, because you are.

> Since you have accepted Christ Jesus as Lord, live in union with him. (Colossians 2:6, GNB)

A married person who continues to act like a single person is going to miss out on many of the blessings of marriage. Similarly, a Christian who fails to draw from their union with Christ is going to miss many of the blessings of that union. New life is meant to be lived; it's meant to be expressed and enjoyed and worked out to such a degree that unbelievers see it and marvel.

How do we bear his fruit in our lives? By not trying. Fruit grow naturally (see Mark 4:26–28). We hinder that process by trying to make things happen in our own strength and understanding. Do that and you'll produce Ishmaels. But learn to rely on his love and trust in the Father's pruning and you will bear his fruit effortlessly.

The many benefits of union

Let us give thanks to the God and Father of our Lord Jesus Christ! For in our union with Christ he has blessed us by giving us every spiritual blessing in the heavenly world. (Ephesians 1:3, GNB)

You may know that you are blessed in your new life, but you may not know that 100 percent of your blessings come as the result of being one with Christ. Let us consider some of these blessings, starting with salvation. What exactly is the basis for your salvation? It is your union with Christ. You are not saved because you said the magic words of a sinner's prayer. You are saved because you are one with the Lord and his saving life is your life. Paul said he endured all things so others may "obtain the salvation that is *in Christ Jesus*" (2 Timothy 2:10).

We mislead people when we sell salvation as a ticket to heaven. It's not that it's wrong, it's just woefully incomplete. Salvation is not about being put into a lifeboat but being put into Jesus (Ephesians 1:13). Besides, those in lifeboats aren't really saved. They still need to be rescued. This is why Christians with a lifeboat mentality are anxious and fearful. Bobbing around in the ocean of their insecurity, they have no assurance that they are actually saved. Perversely, they fear Judgment Day more than the average sinner. Not us. We are as secure as the Savior himself. We fear no condemnation because there is no condemnation to those who are *in Christ Jesus* (Romans 8:1).

Later in this book we are going to see that because of God's grace we have been made holy and righteous. How is it that we dare to call ourselves a holy people? It is because Jesus is holy and we are in him. Paul said of the most misbehaving bunch of Christians in the Bible that they were "sanctified *in Christ Jesus*" (1 Corinthians 1:2). So were you. When did this happen? It didn't happen when you attended that holiness retreat. It happened when you were dipped into the Holy One by the Holy Spirit. Some Christians act holier-than-thou, as if there were levels to holiness, but there's only one level and it's his level. Jesus is your holiness. You don't have to sweat your way to sainthood for you are already numbered among the saints *in Christ Jesus*.[6]

> Christ was without sin, but for our sake God made him share our sin in order that *in union* with him we might share the righteousness of God. (2 Corinthians 5:21, GNB)

The Good News Bible is not the most literal translation but it absolutely nails it when it conveys the idea of shared righteousness. How can we presume to call ourselves righteous? Because the vine is righteous and he shares his righteousness with his branches. How could he not? Since we are inextricably joined together it is meaningless to speak of one kind of righteousness for the vine and another for the branches. We are just as righteous as he is.

These New Testament revelations exceed the wildest dreams of the Old Testament prophets. Prophets like Isaiah and Jeremiah spoke of the righteous *One* and foresaw a righteous *Branch*.[7] They could not imagine that the Branch would become a vine reproducing itself in millions upon millions of little righteous branches. They saw the coming Christ but not the coming Christians who now carry his life and nature and who have been made the very righteousness of God *in Christ Jesus*.

The blessings of our union are many and I could keep going. Indeed, I will. Like Paul, my prayer is that you will have "a deeper understanding of every blessing which we have in our life *in union* with Christ" (Philemon 1:6, GNB).

How is it that we can live free from the demands of the law?
The Gentile believers who walked in this revelation scandalized
the Jews of the first century. "Who are these Johnny-come-latelies
who dare to claim all the blessings of the law while ignoring all of
its curses?" We are the happy branches of a vine who fulfilled the
law on our behalf. It's really not that complicated. Since the vine is
blessed, his branches must be blessed too. How could it be otherwise?

What about our authority? On what grounds can we call ourselves the head and not the tail? What right do we have to speak
to storms, cast out demons, and heal the sick? All together now —
it is because we are wedded to the One who holds all authority in
heaven and earth. Our bodies may be here, but we are seated
together with God in heaven *in Christ Jesus* (Ephesians 2:6).

We read that Jesus sits waiting for his enemies to be placed
under *his* feet (1 Corinthians 15:25). We also read that the God of
peace will soon crush Satan under *our* feet (Romans 16:20). So
under whose feet is the enemy going? His. Ours. All of the above.
Since we are in union with the One who has defeated the enemy,
we are already victorious *in Christ Jesus*. Our part is simply to
stomp.

The list of benefits goes on and on. We have forgiveness in
him. We are perfect in him. We are reconciled through him. Peace,
joy, provision, and everything besides, comes to us through our
union with Jesus Christ.

For in union with Christ you have become rich in all
things ... (1 Corinthians 1:5, GNB)

Do you see it yet? You are mightily blessed because of your
union with the Lord. Your needs are not met through prayer,
fasting, and Bible study. Neither are they met by sowing into this
ministry or signing up for that class. Whatever your need, your
abundant supply is found *in Christ Jesus*.

And my God will meet all your needs according to his
glorious riches *in Christ Jesus*. (Philippians 4:19)

The purpose of union

The blessings of our union with Christ are many and wonderful, but they pale in comparison to the ultimate purpose of union, which is to share in his life. Why did God make us? It was so we could participate in the abundant and overflowing life found within the Godhead. We were created to love and be loved and to enjoy fellowship with the One who made us.

> For your Maker is your husband — the Lord Almighty is his name ... (Isaiah 54:5)

In a word, it's all about Jesus. Jesus is both the means for our union and union's true object. Indeed, Jesus is the Reason for everything. Life lived apart from Jesus doesn't satisfy and doesn't last. Only in him do we live and move and have our being.[8]

Jesus came to give us abundant life, and that life is found in him. Again, we can miss it when we seek the gifts independently of the Giver. Eternal life, for instance, is not more of the same old, broken-down life we inherited from Adam. It is a wholly new life that comes from knowing God and walking in the new way of the Spirit. The difference between the old life and the new is the difference between being lost and found. There is just no comparison.

When Paul said, "I have been crucified with Christ and I no longer live, but Christ lives in me" (Galatians 2:20), he was rejoicing in his co-baptism and resurrection with Jesus. This is the triumphant shout of a man who has found his place in the larger order of things. Paul understood there is no real life outside of Christ and those who seek to live independently on the basis of their own wits and resources ultimately lose their true selves. But when you abandon yourself totally to him, then you discover who you really are. Then you really live.

The gospel of union

Perhaps you originally came to Christ on account of some need. It may have been a need for healing, forgiveness, or simply to get a ticket in to heaven. Whatever your need, God is faithful and generous. Receive from the abundant provision of his grace and be blessed. But then brace yourself for a blessed shock. The Giver is greater than his gifts. The Blesser is infinitely lovelier than his blessings.

The gospel is not an advertising brochure for the treasures of the kingdom. The gospel is the thrilling revelation that the Lover of your soul desires to share his life in wedded union with you forever. For those who believe it, the gospel is the joyful declaration that right now and forever more, you are in perfect union with him. Your days of restless wandering are over, for in Christ you have already found your eternal rest. In Christ, you are already home.

5

Accept one another, then, just as Christ accepted you ....
(Romans 15:7)

A C C E P T E D

When I was in high school, an opportunity came to represent my state on a national televised quiz show. The smartest students from all over the country were going to compete to determine the national champion. I was dead keen to sign up. This was my chance to win fame and glory, to break out of the pit of teenage anonymity. At school I was a Nobody, but this quiz show was going to turn me into a Somebody.

To get accepted onto the show, I first had to compete against dozens of bright students from my own school, then I had to beat hundreds of others students from across the state. A few days after the testing and interviews with the show's producers, my school principal pulled me out of class to let me know I had been selected to represent the school and the state on TV. The excited man nearly shook my arm off.

For about a week I was king of the world. Classmates high-fived me and students I barely knew whispered my name as I passed them in the corridors. I had won the respect of my peers by answering a few trivia questions and being quick on the buzzer. You can imagine the boost that sort of achievement gives to a young man's ego.

It didn't last long. In the first round of the national competition I was soundly defeated by a faster and brighter student. In less than 22 minutes of airtime my reputation changed from state champ to quiz show loser, and I fell from the high place of acceptance to the low place of rejection.

Such is life.

Every single one of us has experienced the highs of acceptance and the lows of rejection. As social creatures we were created with the need to be accepted. We hunger for approval and approbation. God put these needs and desires within us so that we might look to him to fulfill those needs. When we don't—when we seek to get our need for acceptance met outside of him—we can literally hand our lives away.

Living by the expectations of others

In this world acceptance comes at a price. If you want to be accepted you have to perform, you have to deliver, you have to shine. You have to be first in and best dressed. You have to close the deal and make the sale. You have to woo the girl and win the crowd. You have to dazzle the customer and impress the boss. You have to press the buzzer quicker than the next guy. In other words, our acceptance is determined by other people. To win respect and approval, you have to play by the rules others have set. You have to conform to their standards.

Live like this and your legitimate need for acceptance will dictate what you do, where you live, how you talk, even what you eat, drink, and wear. Your life will be defined by other people's expectations. This is what I mean when I say we can hand our lives away. In our desire for acceptance we sign up for courses we're not really interested in, we take on jobs that suck the life out of us, and we get cozy with those who don't love us.

If acceptance is the carrot, then the fear of rejection is the stick. The fear of rejection causes us to live dull, riskless lives, to stay silent when we might speak out, and to hold back when we might launch forth. In our desire to avoid rejection we sign up for nothing, we stick with jobs we have outgrown, and we get cozy with no one.

The desire to ascend to the high places of acceptance and avoid the valleys of rejection is one of the strongest reasons we do the things we do.

Left out of the in-group

Every manmade religion trades in the market for performance-based acceptance. For Christians this unholy trade is based on the lie that says you have to work to make yourself acceptable and pleasing to God. You've got to toe the line, do what you're told, and make whatever sacrifices are currently in vogue with those up the front. Some churches prescribe codes of conduct and assign people to accountability groups to make sure they keep them. Others, who may scoff at this Old Testamenty idea of writing down rules, don't hesitate to impose with equal fervor their own unwritten expectations defining "acceptable" behavior. In either case, newcomers quickly learn what one must do to be considered "a good Christian" or "one of us." Those who conform are welcomed (Acceptance! Hooray for me!), while those who don't are marginalized (Rejection! Dear God no!).

Performance-based acceptance is a diabolical game with no winners and plenty of losers. Those who fail to perform are made to feel like nobodies while those who get the gold stars can end up further from grace than when they started. This happens when the applause of men deafens them to the voice of the Father that says, "You don't need to do any of this to please me."

Life's winners can be its biggest losers if they become addicted to the feeling of being special that comes from accomplishment. "You love me, you really love me." In the pursuit of that high they sacrifice themselves and their families on the altar of achievement. They may even come to define themselves in terms of their results or, in Christianese, their "fruit." They become number-worshippers, their conversations littered with references to how many people God is touching through their ministry. "God is really using me. I must be a Somebody."

When things turn sour and their success evaporates, they no longer know who they are. "I thought I was a minister but my ministry's gone. Who am I?" What began as a legitimate quest for acceptance and approval ultimately robs them of their identity.

The end of the slave trade

The market for acceptance and affirmation is a slave market. It perpetuates a system of human sacrifice based on envy and selfish ambition. It dehumanizes all who trade in it and fosters a distorted image of our heavenly Father as a loveless, scorekeeping judge.

To end this unholy trade it is essential that we preach the gospel of acceptance, and here it is: The love of the Lord is not for sale. Like everything with grace, his acceptance and approval is a free gift that comes to us through Christ alone:

To the praise of the glory of his grace, by which he made us accepted in the Beloved. (Ephesians 1:6, NKJV)

This verse is fantastically good news for those who want no part in the acceptance game. Look at the first part of that verse. Does it say, "To the praise of the glory of *your service*?" It does not. His acceptance of you is to the praise of the glory of *his grace*. Isn't that wonderful?

But wait, it gets better. Look at the middle part of that verse. "He made us accepted." His acceptance is not something you ever need strive for; you already have it. What relief! What freedom!

But wait, there's more. Look at the final part of the verse: "in the Beloved." This is referring to Jesus. God's acceptance comes to you on account of his Son. So if you want to know just how acceptable you are to God, you only have to look at the One called Beloved.

On the day Jesus was baptized, a voice from heaven declared, "This is my Beloved Son in whom I am well pleased" (Matthew 3:17, NKJV). Do you know how much ministry success Jesus had accomplished before God spoke those words? None. According to the gospel writers, Jesus had not done a blessed thing. He had preached no sermons, healed no sick, and raised no dead. And yet God said, "I am well pleased with him." That's acceptance such as the world does not know. That is the unconditional affirmation of heaven.

What pleases the Lord?

You may have heard preachers say "find out what pleases the Lord" (Ephesians 5:10). This is usually presented as one of life's big questions, as though we need to trawl through the Bible on a learn-everything-that-pleases-God quest and then do it.

But we already know what pleases the Lord. He told us at the River Jordan. It's Jesus. There is nothing more pleasing to God the Father than God the Son. Jesus is not competing for his Father's acceptance and favor. He is not in a three-way contest with the law and the prophets. On the Mount of Transfiguration Peter wanted to put up three tents honoring the different ministries but God put the spotlight squarely on Jesus:

> This is my beloved Son in whom I am well pleased; hear him! (Matthew 17:5b, NKJV)

And what does Jesus say? "Come to me all who are weary of trying to please others and all who are tired of trafficking in the market for acceptance and I will give you rest" (see Matthew 11:28).

Grace accepts the unacceptable

When Jesus came to earth he shocked everyone by refusing to play the acceptance game. In those days there were rules that disqualified people from approaching God on the basis of behavior, gender, ethnicity, and health. For instance, if you were a sinful, foreign woman with leprosy, you were about as far from God as it was possible to get. Then Jesus showed up and made a beeline for sinners, foreigners, women, and lepers. It's almost as if his intent was to show us that grace is superior to the law. Think about that: The law excludes but grace includes. The law rejects but grace accepts. The law draws lines between us and them, but grace tears down dividing walls.

It's law or grace. Which do you prefer?

Jesus received everyone who came to him: tax collectors, prostitutes, Romans, Samaritans, the mentally unstable, the physically handicapped, and children. He even had dinner with the odd Pharisee or two. Imagine that. Even intolerant, religious wingnuts were accepted by Jesus.

Jesus accepted the unacceptable and loved the unlovable to reveal his Father's gracious heart of acceptance. God is not willing that any should perish. His desire is to have every single one of his lost children come home.

Evangelists talk a lot about receiving Jesus but the good news begins with the announcement that Jesus receives you. It is his acceptance of you that makes the difference. In the eyes of the law you were disqualified by sin, but in the eyes of the Father you have been qualified by grace. You were far away, but in Christ Jesus you have been brought near. You were unacceptable but he has made you accepted in the Beloved.

How did this happen? The moment you opened the door of your heart to Jesus, the favor and acceptance of heaven came flooding into your life. When the Son moved in you instantly became just as acceptable and pleasing to the Father as Jesus is.

What pleases the Lord? It is faith in Jesus. It is resting in his finished work even as the world tries to seduce you back into the dog-eat-dog culture of competition. It is sitting at his feet even as the Marthas of ministry pressure you into doing your part. It is receiving others with the same grace and favor that Jesus Christ received you.

Grace equals acceptance

The grace of God is the key to understanding his divine acceptance. If you see grace as merely a ticket into the kingdom — it gets you through the front door, nothing more — then you're going to be susceptible to the lie that says you have to work to please your Father. You will feel the pressure to prove your salvation by doing all the things Christians are regularly told to do. "You've got to bear fruit. You've got to witness to your neighbors. You've got to make every meeting and support every church activity." This is just nuts. This is no different from how the world works. Instead of bringing the grace-based freedom of heaven to earth we're trying to export our performance-based religion to heaven. Guess what? Heaven's not buying.

Grace does not merely get you through the front door; grace takes you all the way into the throne room and sits you down at the right hand of your heavenly Father. Do you understand how gracious that is? Do you appreciate the monumental price Jesus paid to make you acceptable to God? If we truly valued Christ's sacrifice, we would not dare cheapen it by adding our own.

In our own strength nothing we do impresses God. Our very best is simply not good enough. That's the message of the law. But this is also what makes the good news *good*: He has done it all.

Pancake Christians

We are accepted "in the Beloved." Some take this to mean we are only in the kingdom because we have a friend in high places. This is misleading. It's like saying, "God can't stand you personally but as a special favor to Jesus he'll pretend he can't see you." I know, it's silly. Yet some Christians are worried sick that if God really knew the secrets of their hearts he would kick them out in a heartbeat. In order to avoid detection they maintain such a low profile you could mistake them for pancakes. Others wear masks because they fear rejection. "If you knew who I really am, you wouldn't love me." Well guess what. God knows you better than you know yourself and he still loves you.

Genuine acceptance is based on knowledge. You can't truly accept someone unless you know them and God knows you. He knows everything you have ever done and everything you will ever do. He knows your darkest secrets and every skeleton in your closest. He knows what you did last summer and what you're going to do next winter. And despite knowing all this, your heavenly Father still loves you like crazy.

You may be worried that you will disappoint God. It's not going to happen. It is literally impossible to disappoint an all-knowing God. When you make a mistake you may surprise yourself—"I can't believe I did that"—but God is never surprised. Since nothing you do ever catches God off guard, rest assured that you can never disappoint him. When you stumble he responds with unaffected grace: "I knew you were going to do that, but don't worry, I still love you."

Jesus knew ahead of time that Peter was going to deny him and yet Jesus didn't reject Peter. Instead he loved him and prayed for him. Jesus knew ahead of time that Judas would betray him and yet Jesus didn't reject Judas. In the very act of betrayal Jesus called him "friend" signaling that even in that dark moment the door of acceptance remained wide open.[1]

We don't deserve any of this. We have done nothing to merit his favor. If anything, we have done plenty to warrant his displeasure. Yet Jesus reaches out to a sinful world and says, "Open the door and invite me in for dinner."

Jesus' acceptance is mind-boggling. It's like nothing on earth.

God is not your employer

The good news of God's acceptance is not widely preached. You are much more likely to hear about God's high standards than his unmerited favor. It's like Jesus has this list of positive qualities he is looking for in his ideal bride. "She needs to be a good cook, like Martha, and have plenty of good works, like the woman in Proverbs 31. She should have a sense of humor and enjoy long walks on the beach ..."

It's ridiculous. Jesus has no list and if he did, none of us would ever make it. Yet many act as if Jesus was grading them on their performance. They mistake the voice of condemnation for the Lover of their souls: "How much did you pray last week? Five minutes? Oh deary dear. I didn't think I could be disappointed but you disappoint me."

This perverse picture of performance-based acceptance has given rise to a strange situation: While many Christians know that Jesus is the friend of sinners, they don't know that he is the friend of *them*. They don't see themselves as God's friends but his servants. "I'm just a humble doorkeeper in the house of my Lord." No you are not. Jesus didn't suffer and die to increase the size of heaven's household staff. What in the world does God need servants for anyway? The One who spoke the universe into existence is quite capable of doing everything himself.

God is not your divine employer; he is your heavenly Father who loves you. It is imperative that you get this. You have to see yourself as totally accepted by God and basking in his divine and unmitigated pleasure. This is where the rubber of your faith hits the road of his grace. If you don't receive his acceptance, you will waste your life running after something he has already given you.

Your true value

In the market for performance-based acceptance, your value to any organization is defined by your ability to produce. Those who get the results get the recognition. But in the kingdom of God your value is determined by the One who accepts you. Your value is not based on your results or your fruit but your Father's unconditional approval.

God accepts you! (I'll keep banging this drum until I get an "Amen.") Whether you preach a thousand sermons or none at all, your heavenly Father is thoroughly pleased with you. There is nothing you can do to make him more pleased than he already is. Just as your good works don't make you any more pleasing to God, neither do your bad works make you less pleasing. If you yell at the kids and fight with your spouse you are still acceptable. You may need to make peace with your family but you already have everlasting peace with God on account of Jesus.

This is so alien to the way we have been raised that we have trouble believing it. "But I'm a total failure. Look at the mess I have made of my life." And God responds, "You're my beloved child and I am well pleased with you."

Our Father's loving affirmation is completely at odds with the fault-finding messages of this broken world. We are constantly being told, "You're not good enough. You're not smart enough, tall enough, rich enough, or cool enough. Your teeth aren't white enough or straight enough. Your skin is the wrong color, your body is the wrong shape, and you smell bad." Listen to this twaddle long enough and you'll end up a miserable wreck. You'll make yourself susceptible to the seductive lies of advertisers and snake oil salesmen.

If you want a proper estimation of your true worth, don't look at your academic transcripts or your resume and definitely don't look in the mirror. Instead, look to the cross. Jesus loves you more than his own life. That's the message of the gospel and it's the cure for mother wounds, low self-esteem, and all forms of rejection.

Understand that there are different voices all competing to be heard and that you have to choose whom you will heed. On the one hand you have broken people speaking lies about you that really say more about their own brokenness than yours, and on the other you have Almighty God declaring his unconditional acceptance of you. The world finds fault with you and does nothing to help, but God says, "You're mine" and pours out his favor.

Who will you listen to?

Acceptance elevates us

When you know God is pleased with you regardless of your productivity, it will free you from the pressure to perform. When you've heard God say "Yes" to you, it will empower you to say "No" to the unhealthy demands of Pharaoh's whip-cracking taskmasters. If you have been burning the candle at both ends trying to get ahead, a revelation of God's acceptance will bring you to a place of rest. It will get you off the merry-go-round and sit you down in pastures green.

But that doesn't mean you will be idle. Those who wait upon the Lord renew their strength (Isaiah 40:31). Paradoxically, those who have been freed from the need to produce are often the most productive people around. This happens because the loving acceptance of another brings out the best in us, particularly if the *Other* is someone special.

Perhaps you have had the pleasant experience of being accepted by the most beautiful girl in the room or the best man in the house. It is the thrill of being elevated to a higher level. "Really?! You choose me? But you're way out of my league." As nice as that is, it pales in comparison to the lift that comes from being accepted by the Maker of heaven and earth. To the glory of his grace you have been lifted out of the miry clay and seated with him in heavenly places. Talk about your upward mobility.

With God on our side like this, how can we lose? (Romans 8:31b, The Message)

When you realize that God is for you, it gives you boldness. You begin to strut, not out of arrogance but confidence. "God is on my side. How can I lose?" You'll walk into the lion's den with a holy swagger and face the furnace without fear. "God is with me. I will not be burned" (see Isaiah 43:2).

Situations that intimidate the socks off your coworkers won't bother you in the slightest. You'll go in front of performance reviews and interview panels with complete peace and without any desperate need to impress. "My promotion comes from the Lord. If these guys see that, great, if they don't, that's their problem." Secure in your Father's approval, you won't be bothered whether your ministry flourishes or flounders. "It's his church anyway. I'm just pleased to play a part."

But the good news is you won't fail. How can you? When you are confident of your Father's absolute delight in you,

> You'll be on your way up!
> You'll be seeing great sights!
> You'll join the high fliers who soar to high heights.[2]

With all due respect to Dr. Seuss, this is not about the empowerment that comes from self-belief but the divine and uplifting influence of God's mighty grace.

Sons and daughters who are supercharged by their Father's favor shine like stars (Philippians 2:15). Elevated by his love they mount up with wings like eagles. They race against horses and walk on water, living testimonies of the energizing power of his divine acceptance.

The accepting church

Divine acceptance will change the world but before it does it must first change the church. For too long the church has been known as a place of rejection, judgment, and condemnation. This is the inevitable consequence of mixing grace with law and preaching a partial gospel. This mixed message makes the children of God fearful of their heavenly Father, it causes the saints to hang back in the fringes of the kingdom, and it paints a frown on the face of Love.

Can you imagine God the Father frowning at Jesus? Of course not. Then neither is he frowning at you.

In the old covenant they prayed for the day when the Lord would make his face shine upon you, be gracious to you, and give you peace. The good news is that you are living in that day. He is looking at you full in the face and beaming with a galaxy-sized smile. You are the apple of his eye and he rejoices over you with singing.

When we see this it will transform us from the inhospitable church we are to the accepting church we are called to be. "Accept one another, as Christ accepted you" (Romans 15:7). Imagine if we did that. We wouldn't be able to exclude the rabble and the riff-raff from our congregations and communion. Instead, we would have to start making welcome announcements like this:

> We extend a special welcome to those who are single, married, divorced, gay, filthy rich, black and proud, *y no habla Ingles*. We extend a special welcome to those who are newborns, poor as dirt, skinny as a rail, or got a hitch in their git-along. You're welcome here if you're "just browsing," just woke up, or just got out of jail. We don't care if you're more Lutheran than Luther, or more Catholic than the Pope, or haven't been in church since little Sophia's dedication. We offer a special welcome to those who could lose a few pounds, think the earth is flat, work too hard, can't spell, or came because grandma's in town and wanted to go to church. We offer a special welcome to those who could use a prayer right now, are three-times divorced, had religion shoved down your throat as a kid, or got lost in traffic and wound up here by mistake. We welcome those who are in recovery or still addicted. If you blew all your offering money at the dog track, you are welcome here. We welcome tourists, seekers, doubters, bleeding hearts ... and you. Welcome Home![3]

The gospel of acceptance

Freedom is found in the Father's acceptance. When you know beyond all doubt that you are your Daddy's delight, you will be set free from the need to please others. The pressure to perform will lift and the unholy expectations of men will seem ridiculous. *My Father is pleased with me. I don't have to prove a thing!* If thoughts of rejection should enter your head, you will dismiss them without a care. *God is for me! Who can be against me?*

Secure in your Father's favor you will become fearless and bold. You will dine in the presence of your enemies and laugh in the face of adversity. You will dance upon the waves of circumstance and when you are tried by fires of life you shall not be burned.

The gospel is not an invitation to accept Jesus; it is the stunning announcement that he accepts you. Although the law reveals it is impossible for you to make yourself acceptable and pleasing to God, the gospel of acceptance declares that in Christ you have been made acceptable for eternity. Nothing you do can make you more or less pleasing to God than you already are. All this is to the praise of the glory of his grace.

We have been made holy through the sacrifice of the body of Jesus
Christ once for all. (Hebrews 10:10)

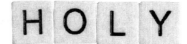

If you were to take a trip to heaven, you might hear the angels
crying, "Holy, holy, holy is the Lord God Almighty."[1] God is holy
but what is holiness? For many years I thought I knew. Then I
realized that what I thought of as holiness did not come close to
describing the Lord. When I found out what holiness really means,
I was stunned. I began to understand why the angels sing.

True holiness is breathtaking. Yet most Christians don't know
what it is. They know they are supposed to be holy or sanctified
but they have been offered an imitation brand of holiness that is a
shadow of the real thing. They have been told sanctification is like
gym membership. "You've got to sign up, make a commitment,
and work at it. Don't expect instant results," the gym instructors
say, "because the process of becoming holy is a work of gradual
development. It takes time and there's no guarantee you'll ever
make it. But keep coming to class and handing over your money
because without holiness no one will see the Lord."

In the pursuit of holiness entire movements have been
launched and countless sermons have been preached and not one
of them has ever succeeded in making anyone holy.

So what is holiness and how do we attain it?

What is holiness?

There are many definitions of holiness. For some, holiness means
the avoidance of sin. This definition is informed by the old covenant law found in the first few books of the Bible. The law contains a list of things you should not do, should not touch, and
should not eat. Back then if you wanted to stay undefiled, you had
to avoid trimmed beards, tattoos, bacon, and lepers.[2]

In the modern world, the list of untouchable items varies but the same basic rule is still observed; to be holy you have to steer clear of contaminating sin. But defining holiness as the avoidance of sin is like defining light as the absence of darkness. Technically it's true, but it's a poor definition. It is defining the thing in terms of something that is not the thing. It doesn't actually tell us what holiness is. Neither does it describe a God who was holy long before there was any sin to avoid. In the beginning, there was no sin, and yet God was just as holy then as he is today. He was unblemished before there were blemishes.

So what is holiness? Some say it is being set apart from the world. "It's coming out from among them and being separate." Okay, but again that's a weak definition. It's like describing God as "not the devil." This interpretation also conveys the idea that God is allergic to sin, which isn't true. His holy grace is greater than our unholy sin.

"But wasn't Jesus said to be undefiled and separate from sinners?" (see Hebrews 7:26). He was, and yet he was also the sinner's friend. His heart was for the unclean, the unhealthy, and the ungodly. The problem with a lot of holiness preaching is that it makes us unfriendly towards sinners. Unlike Jesus, we don't spend any time with them. We dare not. We might catch something.

Others try a more positive spin. "It's not what we're separated *from*, but what we're separated *to*. Holiness is being dedicated to God." Okay, that's fine I guess. But how does this apply to a holy God? Are we saying God is dedicated to himself?

"Holiness is God-fearing godliness." So now we're saying God is godly? That he reveres himself and is Self-fearing?! The mind boggles.

"Holiness means 'worthy of devotion.' A holy God is worthy of our worship." True, God is worthy, and yet the Bible says the angels are also holy. Should we worship them? The saints are holy too. Should we worship ourselves?

See the problem? We don't really know what holiness means. And if you don't know what holiness is, how are you going to heed all those New Testament instructions to "be holy"? How are you ever going to see the Lord?

Okay, we have danced around the target long enough. It's time to zero in on the true meaning of holiness.

The whole meaning of holiness

Holiness means wholeness. To say "God is holy" is to refer to the wholeness, fullness, beauty, and abundant life that overflows within the Godhead. God lacks nothing. He is unbroken, undamaged, unfallen, completely complete and entire within himself. He is the indivisible One, wholly self-sufficient, and the picture of perfection. When the angels sing "Holy is the Lord," they are not admiring him for his rule-keeping or sin avoidance. They are marveling at the transcendent totality of his perfection. To worship God in the beauty of his holiness is to be awestruck by the infinite sweep and scale of his sublimity. It is to become lost in the limitless landscape of his loveliness.

Holiness is not one aspect of God's character; it is the whole package in glorious unity. It is the adjective that precedes all other attributes. Hence, the love of God is a holy love; it is the whole and unrestrained love of the Trinity spilling over into the hearts of humanity. His righteousness is a holy righteousness; it is the habit of right action that flows naturally from One who is in such harmony with himself that he is incapable of acting any other way. His joy is a holy joy; it is the pure and unshadowed delight that accompanies every expression of his love and goodness.

Holiness is hard for us to comprehend because we have never seen its like. We are more familiar with our needs than his fullness, our brokenness than his wholeness. When the writer of Hebrews said, "Without holiness no one will see the Lord," he was not making a threat but describing a fact (Hebrews 12:14). Our experience in a sick and broken world has not equipped us to relate to One who is healthy and whole. We don't even speak the same language. Our native tongue is the language of lack and longing but Jesus came speaking the language of abundant life. "Be perfect," said the Holy One. The word for "perfect" means "complete" or "full grown."[3] It means "whole." Jesus was saying, "Be whole as your Father in heaven is whole." He was calling us to the life that is his.

The holy life of the Holy One

Jesus is the only one of us who lived undamaged by sin. He walked among the wreckage of fallen humanity as a beacon of wholeness and health.

Jesus knew no sin yet the writer of Hebrews tells us he "learned obedience" and was "made perfect."[4] That sounds like a contradiction, as though Jesus started out as a disobedient sinner but came good in the end. Perhaps he signed up for one of those sanctification courses and sweated his way to sinlessness. No, that didn't happen. What the writer of Hebrews is saying is that the full beauty and purpose of Jesus' ministry was not realized until the cross. Before he died, his ministry was incomplete or imperfect. But on the cross everything that needed to be done to save and sanctify you was accomplished:

> Later, knowing that all was now *completed*, and so that the scripture would be *fulfilled*, Jesus said, "I am thirsty." ... When he had received the drink, Jesus said, "It is *finished*." With that, he bowed his head and gave up his spirit. (John 19:28,30)

Look at the words used in that passage to describe the climax of Jesus' ministry; *completed, fulfilled, finished*. If Christ is your life, this is the sort of language you should use to describe your own pursuit of holiness: *completed, fulfilled, finished*. You don't have to work to become holy; you have been made holy through Jesus' completed, fulfilled, and finished work on the cross:

> For by one offering he hath perfected forever them that are sanctified. (Hebrews 10:14, KJV)

An astonishing thing has happened. Through an act of his will and by the sacrifice of his body you have been sanctified for all time. This was the purpose of his ministry. He was numbered among the transgressors so that you might be numbered among the holy.[5]

In all history only one person ever succeeded in sanctifying himself, and he did it on your behalf. Jesus said "I sanctify myself, that they too may be truly sanctified" (John 17:19). Was Jesus-as-high-priest made perfect on the cross? Yes! Then you are well and truly sanctified. You are like the newlywed who wakes up on the first day of the honeymoon and says, "I don't feel married — this is all new to me — but because of what happened yesterday I am well and truly married." This is not a gradual process requiring many years of slow laborious self-improvement. Just as you are either married or unmarried, you are either holy or unholy. The moment you said "I do" to the Holy One you entered into union with him and became just as holy as he is.

"Really? I'm not sure I can believe that, Paul." Well the good news for you is that the unbelieving spouse is sanctified by the other.

"But I don't feel holy; in fact, I feel distinctly unholy." Stop living on the basis of your feelings and align your thinking with God's word. Go to language school if you must and acquaint yourself with the new vocabulary of holiness. You are not a sorry sinner in need of sanctification; you are a holy saint and the temple of the Holy Spirit. Can you imagine the Holy Spirit living in an unholy dump? Of course not. Yet he lives in you. You must be holy.

"You said holiness means completeness or wholeness. But I come from a broken family and a broken marriage. I feel incomplete." A husband or wife won't complete you and neither will raising children. We put unholy pressure on others when we expect them to do what only God can do. "You are complete in him" (Colossians 2:10, NKJV). Jesus completes you. You were broken, but in him you are whole. You were in lack, but he who has Christ lacks no good thing. Your life was a sinful mess, but he gave you beauty for ashes. Isn't that good news?[6]

Practical holiness

Practical holiness is a term to beware of because it often hides a fishhook: "You've got to work at your sanctification. You've got to strive to live by God's holy instructions." This is false advertising.

It is old covenant behavior modification dressed up as a second work of grace—as if the first work of grace was insufficient. Don't fall for it. Jesus has already worked to sanctify you and his work cannot be improved upon.

I sometimes hear from believers who think the law shows us how to live holy. "We are saved by grace and perfected through the law." I tell them this is a recipe for disaster for "the law made nothing perfect" (Hebrews 7:19). Although the law is holy and good, it has no power to make you holy and good. The law is not a *Saints' Guide to Holy Living*; it is a signpost to Jesus.

Others say we are sanctified by works. "We've got to keep the commands of Jesus. We've got to follow the instructions of Paul." Not to get holy you don't. Nothing you do can make you holy.

"Then how do you explain all those New Testament verses calling us to be holy?" Okay, let's look at an example from Paul:

> It is God's will that you should be sanctified: that you should avoid sexual immorality. (1 Thessalonians 4:3)

A gym instructor might use this scripture to tell you that you are not sanctified, that you need to be sanctified, and that the way to get sanctified is to avoid sexual immorality. Such an interpretation comes straight out of the old covenant. Paul is not saying that at all. He is saying, "You are holy, therefore be holy." See the difference? One says do to become, the other says do because you are.

Behavior follows identity. A broken and damaged person who tries to live holy is like a fish in a footrace. They are not going to get very far. If they succeed at avoiding one kind of sin (e.g., sexual immorality) you can be sure they will be undone by another (e.g., self-righteous pride).

The avoidance of sin cannot make a broken person whole. But if you have already been made whole by Jesus and have learned to look to him to meet all your needs, you will avoid sin effortlessly. The good news is that even if you fail, you are still holy. Do you understand this? Since nothing you did made you holy in the first place—you were sanctified through his will and his sacrifice—nothing you do can make you unholy. Thank you, Jesus!

Learning to live holy

Holy living is normal for holy people. It's what holy people do. This is why the New Testament writers consistently followed the pattern of establishing identity before giving instructions on how to live holy. Paul was a master at this. Just look how he begins his letter to the misbehaving Corinthian Christians: "To those sanctified in Christ Jesus and called to be holy" (1 Corinthians 1:2). See the pattern? Identity first (you are sanctified in Christ Jesus); behavior second (so be holy).

It was the same message for the Thessalonians: "You are all sons of the light, so act like it" (see 1 Thessalonians 5:5–6).

Similarly, Peter exhorts us to "be holy in all you do" (1 Peter 1:15), before reminding us we are a holy priesthood and a holy nation (1 Peter 2:9).[7]

One more time for emphasis: We don't act holy to become holy but because we are holy. It is in our new nature to live whole, to speak with a wholesome tongue, and to think the best of others. A child of a holy God who acts in an unholy manner is a hypocrite. They are acting contrary to their true nature. This can happen if they have been fed a steady diet of lies and laws: "You're not holy. Follow the commands of God and strive to get holy." It can also happen if they are ignorant of their true identity, if they have been told, "You're an unholy work in progress." Perversely, this sort of holiness preaching does nothing to promote holiness. Instead it inflames sin and stirs up the flesh in a vain attempt to overcome it. It teaches people to trust in themselves rather than the unmerited favor of God who has sanctified them.

What is practical holiness? It is learning to walk in the reality that Jesus has made you whole and given you everything you need for life and godliness. It is learning to function as God intended you to function.

Holiness is not something to strive for; like salvation, it's something you have and work out. Think of a toddler learning to walk. The toddler has within them everything they need to walk, run, and jump. They just need to work it out. That's how it is with holiness. We are whole—God has given us everything we need in Jesus—we just need to learn how to live whole. It's a new and wonderful experience for us. We have not been this way before but with our eyes fixed on Jesus the Holy One, we cannot fail.

The end of the race

Much damage has been done in the pursuit of holiness. We have been told we are competing in an endurance race with the implication that the weak among us probably won't make it. "So try harder or die trying!" In the name of sanctification we have been sold tickets for an endless pilgrimage to an unknown destination without any guarantees we'll ever arrive. But the good news of grace declares that in Christ you have arrived already. The Christian race starts at the finish line.

So cancel the sanctification classes, throw out the gym membership, and stop sweating for Jesus. Stop pretending you can finish what he started. Instead, be confident that he who began a good work in you will carry it on to completion. And don't be discouraged by your mistakes. When you stumble, you are still holy. You are progressing from glory to glory and strength to strength. Know that your Papa-God has delight in his eyes as he watches you take your first steps.

The gospel of holiness

The gospel of holiness is almost never preached in its full glory. The result is that many Christians still struggle with sin despite their best efforts to avoid it. They are like patients who won't leave the hospital because they think they are still broken. They do not know that Dr. Jesus has made them whole.

The gospel is not a sign-up sheet for sanctification classes. The gospel is the definitive announcement that in Christ you are holy indeed. Jesus took your broken down and raggedy old life and gave you his whole life in exchange. You have been called to the adventure of discovering who you are in Christ and presenting yourself as a holy offering to the Lord. You are a living and beautiful testimony of the transforming power of his holy grace. Holiness, or wholeness, is the very definition of abundant life. Such is the life you already have in him.

Ye were declared righteous, in the name of the Lord Jesus...
(1 Corinthians 6:11, YLT)

R I G H T E O U S

Several years ago I visited a church to hear a preacher from out of town. The guest preacher opened with a question. "How many people here know they are righteous?" Hundreds of hands went up. Virtually everyone in the room knew that in God's eyes they were righteous. The preacher got everyone to put their hands down before following up with another question. "How many people *feel* righteous?" This time almost no hands went up.

I guess what I saw in that meeting is true of Christians everywhere. Most have some idea that they have right-standing before God, but in their hearts they don't feel it. It's not a truth that has sunk in. It just sits there on the surface waiting to be prodded with leading questions like the one asked by the guest preacher. "Am I righteous? Sure, I guess so. Everyone else has their hand up so I had better raise mine." But deep down they are unsure. They don't know exactly where they stand with God. And since they are not resting in his righteousness, they are seeking to establish their own. By that I mean they are constantly trying to do the right thing. They are trying to choose the right course, the right job, the right spouse, and they are trying live right before God.

There is nothing wrong with wanting to do the right thing. The problem is they often don't know the right thing to do. "Should I choose A or B? What does God say?" Their sincere desire to do right combined with their inability to tell how things will turn out leaves them feeling apprehensive and insecure. "Did I make the right choice?" And when their best laid plans go awry they become perplexed. "How did I end up here? Where did I go wrong?"

Those who don't feel righteous feel anxious. They lack real peace. Of course we don't base our faith on our feelings but feelings should follow faith as surely as peace and joy follow righteousness.

A lack of peace is a byproduct of having to constantly justify one's existence as a Christian. It's the result of living with the mentality that says, "I've got to do my bit. I've got to bear fruit. It's expected of me." People who think like this go to church, attend every conference, and read the latest books because they are looking for someone to tell them what to do. "Have I done enough? Am I good enough?" They are on a righteousness-quest. Like the rich young ruler they are asking, "What good thing must I do to inherit eternal life?"

Since this is the latest book, I don't want to disappoint you. I am going to tell you what you must do to inherit eternal life. Nothing. There is nothing you *can* do. It's an inheritance, a gift passed down from God to his children.

The gift of righteousness

Why is the good news still news for so many? Because as I saw in that meeting, most believers have not heard that the righteousness you and I both need comes to us as a free gift from the Lord. There is simply no way to be righteous other than to receive the gift of his righteousness by faith:

> In the gospel a righteousness from God is revealed, a righteousness that is by faith from first to last. (Romans 1:17a)

The bad news of the law proves you can never be good enough to impress God on your own merits, but the good news of grace declares that he offers you his righteousness as a free gift, no strings attached. This is so simple many miss it. They sail right past the unwrapping of the gift and onto the tidy up. They have no time to sit at the feet of Jesus and receive; they've got cakes to bake and sermons to preach. Ask them how they feel and they will respond, "Tired." Listen to their prayers and you will hear them say, "Lord, don't you care that my brothers and sisters have left me to do all this work by myself?" (see Luke 10:40).

As any child knows, there are only two things you can do with a gift; you can receive it or you can reject it. You can say, "Thank you Jesus, this is exactly what I need." Or you can say, "Oh no, Jesus, let me give you an offering instead. Look at all I am doing for you. Are you impressed?" Only the first response pleases the Lord.

One thing you must never do with a gift, and especially a priceless gift, is insult the giver by trying to pay for it. This is what the Jews of Paul's day were attempting to do and it broke his heart:

Brothers, my heart's desire and prayer to God for the Israelites is that they may be saved. For I can testify about them that they are zealous for God, but their zeal is not based on knowledge. Since they did not know the righteousness that comes from God and sought to establish their own, they did not submit to God's righteousness. (Romans 10:1–3)

Zeal without knowledge of the gospel is a recipe for self-righteous religion. You may be working a hundred hours a week for Jesus but if you have not submitted to the righteousness revealed in the gospel of his grace, your work is for naught. You're stacking firewood and you're not saved.

Self-righteous Sardisians

Many churchgoers are zealous for God with a zeal based on ignorance and unbelief. They are working like slaves but in God's eyes their deeds are incomplete. Like the church in Sardis they have soiled their clothes through works of filthy self-righteousness. What is the remedy? Like the Sardisians, they need to remember what they heard (the gospel), heed it, and start making different choices.[1] They need to stop banking on their own futile attempts at right living and submit to God's righteousness.

I don't think anyone gets out of bed planning to be self-righteous, but self-righteous is what you are if you are trying to impress the Lord with your offerings and sacrifices. When we talk about self-righteousness we tend to think of the Judaizers stalking Paul around the Mediterranean with their sharp circumcision knives. But Martha was a little bit self-righteous and she was literally serving the Lord. She was a one-woman ministry team baking cakes for Jesus.

Martha's problem was not that she was cooking; it's that she wasn't eating. The Chef of Heaven had come to visit and all she wanted to do was make sandwiches for him. That's not how it works. That's back to front. We're not saved or made righteous because we bless him but because he has blessed us. The lesser is blessed by the greater.

Jesus never condemns Martha, that's not his way. But he clearly says her sister Mary made the better choice. Do you see the significance of this? The one who made an impression was the one not trying to impress him. It was not the one who came with the food but the one who came with the appetite.

We can get so caught up in serving the Lord that we forget the Son of Man did not come to be served but to serve (Matthew 20:28). And the main dish on his menu is a hefty helping of righteousness. Hear now the words of the Heavenly Chef:

> Blessed are those who hunger and thirst for righteousness,
> for they will be filled. (Matthew 5:6)

The word for "filled" means gorged, indicating that the Chef of Heaven serves hearty dishes.[2] He is not stingy with grace. When you partake of his righteousness you are filled to the point of satisfaction. When you eat the Bread of Life you get a meal that sustains and nourishes you for eternity. You will never hunger again.

> He who comes to me will never go hungry, and he who
> believes in me will never be thirsty. (John 6:35)

When you have had a hearty meal, the last thing you feel like doing is cooking. You just want to sit and digest and heap praises on the chef. This is a very appropriate response to grace!

How can you tell when a Christian has submitted to God's righteousness? They have a look of well-fed contentment. They are not sweating in the kitchen making sandwiches for Jesus. Neither are they singing discontented songs of hunger and thirst ("Oh feed me Jesus"). Instead, they are pointing hungry people to the Bread of Life by proclaiming the gospel of his satisfying righteousness.

The importance of doing nothing for Jesus

I wasn't being glib before when I said you must do nothing. I'm a grace preacher, I rarely use the word "must." But as far as righteousness is concerned, you really must do nothing. Anything you do to help the Lord in matters of justification will be utterly disastrous. We are justified by faith alone. Period.[3]

Paul said his zealous Jewish brothers did not submit to God's righteousness but sought to establish their own. The operative word here is "submit." Think of a swimmer drowning in the ocean. To be saved he must completely submit to the lifeguard who would rescue him. If he panics and tries to save himself, he will only make the lifeguard's job more difficult.

A few weeks ago I heard a story about a Navy Search and Rescue swimmer who went to the aid of a downed aviator. The aviator began to flail and flounder making the situation dangerous for both himself and his would-be rescuer. The rescue swimmer responded by diving down deeper into the water to get away and to wait for the aviator to give up struggling. In other words, he withdrew from the scene until the aviator exhausted himself.

This is exactly how it is with us and Jesus. We are saved by trusting in him, and we must do nothing to help. Trying to help only makes things worse and leaves us exhausted. And yet, we try. Ever since Adam took up sewing to hide his sin, it has been the nature of the flesh to take control and try and fix things. *I can save myself from drowning.* This is why we should thank God for the magnificent law which reveals the hopelessness of our situation. *But you're in the middle of the ocean! You can't swim that far.* And then thank him even more for good news of his grace that saves us. *Jesus the Savior is here. Stop struggling and submit to his righteousness.*

The first day of summer

When I was in school, my favorite moment in the year was the minute the last exam finished. "Time's up, pens down. Please remain seated until your paper is collected." Can you remember the sweetness of that moment? All the work and the study were behind you; all the tests had been done. Into your mind came one of the sunniest thoughts a young person can have: *School's out for summer!*

This is how it is for the believer when the gospel of righteousness takes root in their heart. The first reaction is one of sweet relief. "Really? Jesus did it all? I don't have to work to impress him? I can stop studying for the exam? Oh happy day!" Many are dreading the final exam. The good news is there is no exam. Jesus already took it on your behalf, and guess what? He passed. *School's out forever!*

> For he made him who knew no sin to be sin for us, that we might become the righteousness of God in him. (2 Corinthians 5:21, NKJV)

You've got to love the math of the new covenant: How many sins did Jesus commit before he was made sin? None. And how many righteous acts did you do before you were made righteous? None. God did it all! The moment you put your faith in Jesus, you were stamped "righteous" for all time and eternity. At one time you were unrighteous, but you were washed, you were sanctified, and you were declared righteous in the name of the Lord (1 Corinthians 6:9–11).

What does it mean to be righteous? It means you have had a complete renovation, a Holy Spirit renewal, an entire rebuild. You have been straightened out. You are no longer the crooked person you used to be. Whereas in Adam you had bent inclinations that led you towards sin no matter how hard you tried to avoid it, in Christ you are inclined to walk straight and true. You have a Holy Ghost gyroscope inside you that keeps you stabilized and on course. Your desire is to please the Lord. I'm not saying you are incapable of sinning. It's just that sinning no longer appeals.

Neither does it satisfy. When you do occasionally sin it bothers the socks off you — "I wish I hadn't done that" — testifying that this sort of behavior is contrary to your new nature.

"But Paul, if I'm so righteous, how come the Holy Spirit keeps convicting me of my sin?" Actually, he never does that. That's an extra-Biblical myth that needs to be busted. Adam didn't need God's help in recognizing his sin and neither do we. Any guilt you have over wrongdoing comes from a condemning source and not the one called Comforter.[4] There is no condemnation — not now, not ever — to those who are in Christ Jesus.

The Comforter's conviction

Jesus said the Holy Spirit would seek to convince us of our righteousness (John 16:8–10). When do you most need convincing of your righteousness in Christ? It is when you are feeling unrighteous. It is when you have just sinned.

When you sin the Holy Spirit will seek to remind you that you are still righteous because you are in Christ the Righteous One.

I appreciate this is completely different to the message many of us have heard (and some of us have preached). We have been told the Holy Spirit is like a heavenly cop who issues warnings whenever we stray. But that's not what Jesus said. He said the Holy Spirit would "glorify me" (that's Jesus), guide us into all truth (also Jesus), and convince us of our righteousness (Jesus again). The Holy Spirit is not closing his eyes to your sin; he is trying to open your eyes to Jesus. Just as a gyroscope in a plane will always reveal the true horizon, the Holy Spirit will always point you to the Righteous One. He will always encourage you to fix your eyes on Jesus.

> Having been declared righteous, then, by faith, we have peace toward God ... (Romans 5:1, YLT)

Do you know why so many believers have no peace in their relationship with God? They would tell you it is because God is angry with them and their sin, but the real reason is they are ignorant of him and his righteousness. In the kingdom, peace always follows righteousness. If you are more conscious of your sin than his righteousness, you will never enjoy peace with God.

The church has an unhealthy obsession with sin. We spend our lives watching out for sin, resisting sin, fighting sin, hiding sin, running from sin, owning up to sin, talking about sin, turning from sin, and hopefully, overcoming sin. With so much emphasis on sin, guilt, and shame, is it any wonder so many of us don't feel righteous? We need the ministry of the Holy Spirit now more than ever.

First things first

Jesus said, "Seek the kingdom and his righteousness first" (see Matthew 6:33). First means first. First does not mean second. Jesus knew if we sought his righteousness second, say, after we'd gotten ourselves all cleaned up and sorted out, it would never happen. Sin-conscious people don't seek his righteousness; they hide behind fig leaves.

We need to change our thinking. We need to put off the old self and "put on the new self, created to be like God in true righteousness and holiness" (Ephesians 4:24). God has done his bit—he has made us new—but we have to put it on. We have to start walking and talking like righteous people. The righteous are supposed to live by faith. When you sin it takes absolutely no faith to feel unrighteous and unforgiven. It takes faith to look at the cross, listen to the Holy Spirit, and confess, "I messed up, but because of Jesus I am still righteous!"

We don't know how good we've got it. In the Old Testament people were labeled righteous if they acted righteously, but you are righteous by design. In the old, righteousness was temporary. You could be righteous on Sunday and unrighteous on Monday.[5] But you have been created to be like God in true righteousness. Do you realize what this means? You are truly and eternally righteous. Your behavior does not come into it. Just as your righteous deeds did not make you righteous, your unrighteous deeds do not make you unrighteous. Don't you see how liberating that is? Instead of wasting time worrying about sin, we can get on with the joyful business of living well and living right.

The paralysis of analysis

Another sign that some don't appreciate the gift of righteousness is anxiety regarding the Lord's will. "What should I do? What does God want me to do with my life?" In Hong Kong I met plenty of Christians who were bouncing around Asia in a quest to divine the Lord's will for their lives. Many of these dear people were living in a state of self-inflicted paralysis. They had put life on hold and were afraid to make choices in case they got it wrong. "What if I miss it?" How can you miss it when you have already hit it?

God's word and the Holy Spirit are declaring together that you are truly righteous. This means your desires are righteous, your dreams are righteous, and your deeds are righteous. To paraphrase Proverbs 12:5, "The plans of the righteous are right." If you want to make a cup of tea, then that is a righteous act. Go and make a righteous cup of tea!

Righteous deeds are what righteous people do. I am not saying you are incapable of dumb choices, and there is no such thing as righteous wrongdoing. But when you abandon yourself completely to his love trusting in the gift of his righteousness, your choices will all be good. Since Jesus has already won, in him you cannot lose.

And now, children, stay with Christ. Live deeply in Christ. Then we'll be ready for him when he appears, ready to receive him with open arms, with no cause for red-faced guilt or lame excuses when he arrives. Once you're convinced that he is right and righteous, you'll recognize that all who practice righteousness are God's true children. (1 John 2:28–29, The Message)

We don't practice righteousness to become God's children; we practice righteousness because we *are* his children. Like our Father we are bona fide, qualified, righteousness practitioners. You should get a framed certificate to remind you. In fact, you should get ten certificates, one for each chapter of this book. Hang them in the living room and they'll be great conversation starters.

You are going to have to trust God that your dreams and desires are righteous. Better still, learn to see the desires of your
heart as God-given seeds planted by him. If your passion is to be a
trampoline tester then go be a righteous trampoline tester. If that
is the God-given desire of your heart it would be a mistake for you
to be anything else.

Living deeply in Christ

One of the greatest failures of the modern church is that we have
defined career success in terms of formal ministry. The message
many young people hear is this: If you want to be a Somebody in
the kingdom, you have four choices; pastor or deacon, if you work
well with others, or missionary or evangelist if you don't. Too bad
if you would rather race cars or make noodles. Too bad if the
music you write or the movies you make are not overtly Christian.

I grew up as a pastor's kid. Through that experience and my
own tenure as a pastor I have met and dined with countless
church leaders. In my opinion most of them have ended up in
formal ministry because it was expected of them or because it
seemed like a good idea at the time. Pastoring is a noble occupation and those who do it well should be applauded. But those who
do it poorly and for the wrong reasons need to be set free from an
occupational choice that was uninformed by the gospel of righteousness.

Living up to other people's expectations or trying to be somebody else is not how you live deeply in Christ. I can also guarantee you that God can think of more than four fulfilling occupations
for his children. Since his imagination is unbounded the possibili-
ties are endless. Your prospects are good. It's quite possible you
were put on this earth to do something that has never been done
before.

You are a precious and unique member of his body. There are
things that are easy for you that are hard for others. You feel and
see things differently from other people. These differences are not
accidental. They hint at the flavor or expression of the kingdom
that God has given to you alone. They point to your gifts and we
need them. The world waits to see Christ revealed in you.

There are only two ways we can screw this up; by refusing to participate (God what should I do?) or by reverting back to old habits of Adamic independence (I'm a self-made man). For some the temptation is to do nothing; for others the temptation is to pull the levers and make things happen. But these are inferior ways to live. You were born for greater things. You have been called to shine like the sun. The God who made you righteous and planted righteous desires within you has set you up for success. He has lined up the resources of heaven in anticipation of blessing all the work of your hands.

To reiterate, this is not about divining the Lord's will in advance. This is about knowing and trusting the One who made you the way you are, who even now orders your steps and who swells your heart with God-sized dreams.

So what are you waiting for? Be convinced of your righteousness, fan the gift of God into flame and go for it. Live deeply in Christ and be the person he made you to be. Your future is bright!

> The path of the righteous is like the first gleam of dawn, shining ever brighter till the full light of day. (Proverbs 4:18)

The gospel of righteousness

When you stumble and sin, an old covenant preacher will say, "Look at what you did!" But a new covenant preacher will say, "Look at what *he* did!" An old covenant preacher would have you turn from every sin until you're a dizzy sinner. But a new covenant preacher will release the grace of God that empowers you to sin no more (Titus 2:12).

Under the old covenant you were righteous because of what you did, but in the new you are righteous because of what he did. You are declared righteous, recreated to be like God in true righteousness.

What does God want you to do with the gift of his righteousness? He wants you to receive it, to walk in it, and to rule and reign with him in righteousness.

The gospel is not a list of things you must do to inherit eternal life. It is the blessed announcement that the righteousness you need to enter the kingdom of heaven—the righteousness that exceeds that of the Pharisees and law teachers—comes to us as a free gift through faith.

For you died, and your life is now hidden with Christ in God.
(Colossians 3:3)

D I E D

Why do 90 percent of Christians struggle to receive grace and live
the Christian life? There are two reasons. First, they do not pro-
perly value what Christ accomplished on the cross. Second, they
do not know what happened to *them* on the cross. Every believer
knows that Jesus died on the cross for their sins, but not every
believer knows they died too. Paul says so, again and again. To
the Christians in Colossae; "You died with Christ." To the believers in Rome: "We died with Christ." To the Corinthians: "We all
died."[1]

You may say, "How did this happen? I don't remember the
nails." Well do you remember the chapter on Union? When you
were included in Christ you were baptized into his death. His
death became your death and, as we shall see, this is very good
news indeed.

Your glorious new past

When you got saved you were probably told a lot of wonderful
things about your future. "God has a wonderful plan for your
life." You may have been told some wonderful things about your
present. "We are living in the kingdom now." But you probably
didn't hear many wonderful things about your past. "It doesn't
matter where you've come from or what you've come out of."

In truth, your past matters a great deal. If you think you came
out of Egypt then you may be tempted to go back to Egypt. "I was
born and bred in Egypt and that's where I belong." But when you
see your old life as crucified with Christ, that tie is severed. The
old Egyptian no longer lives and Egypt no longer appeals.

Here is the good news: God is not only the Lord of your present and future, he is also the Lord of your past. When you were born again, he gave you a brand-new life complete with a brand-new past. You have a new history and it began at the cross where you died with Christ.

> I have been crucified with Christ and I no longer live, but Christ lives in me ... (Galatians 2:20a)

Your baptism into his death is just about the most important thing that ever happened to you, yet many Christians are ignorant of it. Ask them about their past and you will hear all the bad things that happened to them and all the dumb choices they made in their old life. Although their intent is to glorify Christ, the reality is they are living in the shadow of someone else's past. Their present is haunted by the ghost of who they used to be.

Just once I would like to hear a testimony like Paul's: "I was born, I did some stuff, then I died. I was crucified with Christ, and the person I used to be no longer lives."

Do you know how many Christians Paul had killed or locked up before he was born again? Neither do I. He never tells us. We know he got mixed up with some bad stuff because he refers to himself as the chief of sinners, and we know he persecuted the church because other people tell us. But aside from one passing mention in Galatians, Paul says nothing about the sins of his past. It's like he doesn't identify with them. It's like he says, "I forget the past" (see Philippians 3:13).

Don't you find this interesting? If Paul came to speak in our churches we would introduce him as a Very Bad Guy who got turned around by Jesus. But Paul has no time for that. The good stuff of his past he considers dung and the bad stuff he barely mentions. Instead he simply says, "I died."

The cure for schizophrenic Christianity

Paul understood that the foundation of our new life with Christ is a revelation that we died with him:

This is a faithful saying: For if we died with him, we shall also live with him. (2 Timothy 2:11, NKJV)

Paul hammered this point in his letters because if you don't know that you have died, then you won't really live. Instead, you will spend your life trying to die; dying to self, dying daily, and crucifying the flesh.

"But isn't following Jesus a matter of dying daily to ourselves and our desires?" Nope. The phrase "die to self" isn't even in the Bible. When Jesus said, "If anyone would come after me he must deny himself and take up his cross and follow me" (Matthew 16:24), he was showing us the way to salvation—it's through the cross. If you would follow Jesus, *then follow Jesus*. Jesus died once and he will never die again. It's the same with us. We were crucified once; we need never be crucified again. You do not need to die daily. Once will do the trick.[2]

The problem with any message on self—even a noble-sounding message on self-denial—is that it promotes *self*. It fuels self-centeredness which lies at the root of all that is wrong with humanity. In the church self-denial is usually packaged as part of the spiritual disciplines. Don't touch, don't taste, don't handle. But in truth it is nothing more than the age-old practice of asceticism, the belief that we can attain spiritual goals by abstaining from physical pleasures. It's the religion of monks and sadhus. I'm not denying the benefits of abstinence; I'm just saying that skipping cheeseburgers won't make you holy and righteous.

The truth is that you can do nothing to save yourself or make yourself pleasing to God. Jesus does it all. True gospel preachers understand this which is why they will never seek to distract you by preaching messages that glorify self or self-effort. They echo Paul who said, "For we do not preach ourselves, but Jesus Christ as Lord" (2 Corinthians 4:5).

Christians who do not know they have died with Christ end up living two lives. On the one hand they are trying to walk in the new life they have received in Christ, but on the other they are trying to reform the old life they inherited from Adam. This is a recipe for misery. No one wants to be one person on Sunday and another on Monday. Live like this and it'll tear you apart.

The cure for schizophrenic Christianity is not to "try harder" or "lift your game" or "follow these ten steps to a new you." It is a revelation that your old self was crucified with Christ. What is your old self? It is the person you used to be before you met Jesus. It is who you were in Adam before you were put into Christ. Paul wrote that "we know that our old self was crucified with him" (Romans 6:6). Look at his choice of words; *was* crucified. Past tense. Done and dusted. Dead and buried.

Do you see how liberating this is? The old man was unfixable. He was broken, corrupt, and completely screwy. He was a slave to sin who lived for himself and no amount of reform could fix him. But the good news is he's dead. That incorrigible old so-and-so was nailed to the cross with Jesus and he no longer lives.

Watchman Nee called this the gospel for Christians: "The self you loathe is there on the cross in Christ."[3] If the average believer could grasp hold of this truth—*I died*—half of our church programs would cease immediately. We would stop trying to reform the old man because *the old man is dead.*

Better than Buenos Aires

If there's one thing I have learned from the movies, it's that there is no problem that can't be solved by faking your own death and fleeing to a new life in South America. Think of a wiseguy who is part of a crime family. He is under pressure from his superiors to risk his life by engaging in criminal activities. At the same time the law hounds him on account of the crimes he has already done. After a while, the wiseguy realizes he is not his own man and life is no fun when you're not free. He begins to long for a new life but finds he is hemmed in on all sides. If he stays with the family he'll likely end up prematurely dead. But if he turns himself in, he'll spend the rest of his days behind bars. Either way, it's a lose-lose scenario. In desperation he begins to make an audacious plan. "South America, here I come."

The lose-lose scenario describes how it was for us when we were part of Adam's family of sinners. We felt the pressure to conform to the ways of the world and live as children of disobedience. At the same time our consciences bore witness to the law in our hearts that we were unrighteous and guilty as sin. After a while we realized we were not in control of our lives and life is no fun when you're not free. We began to long for a new life but found we were hemmed in on all sides. As members of the family of Adam we were captive to our appetites and enslaved to sin. We wanted to do the right thing but we frequently stumbled. We looked to religion for help but found it was a prison. All it offered was the prospect of a lifetime running on the hamster wheel of self-effort. Self-indulgence or self-denial, either way was a lose-lose proposition.

Thankfully, someone told us of God's audacious plan: "Through the cross the world has been crucified to me and I to the world" (Galatians 6:14). And this was no fake death with flaming car crashes and furtive flights to Buenos Aires, but a real bona fide death as genuine as our union with Christ. We really died. Do you realize what this means? It means we are truly and legitimately free:

> For we know that our old self was crucified with him so that the body of sin might be done away with, that we should no longer be slaves to sin—because anyone who has died has been freed from sin. (Romans 6:6-7)

Real life is better than the movies. Our fictional wiseguy will never enjoy his new life in South America for he will always be looking over his shoulder waiting for his old life to catch up with him. Not us. Our old life is dead. There was a funeral, a tomb, and everything. The old has gone and we are now free to walk in newness of life.

Sin is a noun

You may ask, "Then how come I don't feel free? How come I still do the things I don't want to do?"

It will help if you understand who died on the cross. We died but sin didn't die. That old tyrant Sin is still alive and kicking and trying to push us around.

We tend to think of sin as a verb, but in Romans Paul describes sin as a noun. Sin acts like a person. It has lusts and it desires to deceive and dominate us. It's Sin with a capital S.[4] Paul was not referring to our former sinful tendencies but an external personality that seeks to dominate and devour us.

Sin is an ancient and treacherous enemy. Try and defeat Sin in your own strength and you will surely fail. This was Paul's experience. He tried to overcome Sin in the power of his flesh and failed repeatedly. This frustrated him. "I'm doing what I don't want to do. It's not me but Sin operating in me" (see Romans 7:17). Paul wasn't making excuses. Nor was he saying, "The devil made me do it." He was simply pointing out that when we walk after the flesh we are incapable of resisting Sin.

Walking after the flesh is when you attempt to get your needs met independently of God. It's trusting in yourself and living solely from the basis of sensual experience (what you see, hear, touch, etc.). In Paul's case he was trusting in his ability to keep the law. It didn't work. "I thought I was doing okay but when the commandment came, Sin reared its ugly head and I realized I was a lost cause" (see Romans 7:9).

On our own we are just not capable of living the sinless life. We may try and convince ourselves that we're basically good people—"at least I'm better than the wiseguy down the road"— but the law reveals that our best is not good enough. The only way out for us is to die to that law-based life of self-improvement and put our faith in Jesus.[5]

You may say, "I get that. I understand we are not under law but grace. Why, then, do I still sin?"

I suspect the reason why some Christians continue to sin is that they don't know they have been freed from sin. Nobody has told them. So they continue to act in the way they used to act because it has become a habit. They've had a lifetime of practice. Sure, they don't feel good about it but what can they do? Like Paul, they've made an effort to stop sinning and perhaps experienced some short term success, but it's never lasted. They tried and failed, tried and failed, until they just gave up trying. Now they tell themselves they are a work in progress and that nobody's perfect.

That doesn't sound like freedom to me. That just sounds like your old life with added guilt. Who would want that?

Freed but not yet free

It is for freedom that Christ has set us free (Galatians 5:1). Allow me to paint a picture of what Christ-bought freedom looks like.

When you were in Adam you had no choice but to walk according to the flesh. Trusting in your own abilities and walking by sight is what unbelievers call normal life but it's a faithless life. Since anything that is not of faith is sin (Romans 14:23), your former life was inherently sinful. I don't mean to say you were a raging criminal. It's just that you were incapable of pleasing the Lord no matter what you did. You may have been a good sinner or a bad sinner but you were a sinner nonetheless. You were separated from the life of God through your ignorance and unbelief.

But now you are a saint and a sinner no more. You have a new identity, a new life, and a new master. You are no longer a slave to Sin. You now have the freedom to choose how you will walk, either in the old way of the flesh or in the new way of the spirit. But here's the important bit: If you choose to walk in the old way your new life will resemble your old one. This is why some Christians are still bound. They have left Egypt but Egypt hasn't left them. They are still thinking like slaves and heeding the voice of their old master.

It certainly doesn't help matters when these precious brothers and sisters are told that their sinful behavior proves they still possess a sinful nature or an innate tendency to sin. This is simply not true. Your old self was crucified. Any sinful nature you once had has been cut off, and that circumcision was not done by the hands of men (Colossians 2:11). You are one with the Lord. You do not have two natures dueling for control inside you. You are a partaker of the sinless life and divine nature of Jesus Christ.

So how do we partake? How do we walk in this new way of life and resist the temptation to sin? The wrong way is the old way. It's trusting in the might of Adam and striving in the flesh to be an overcomer. It is telling ourselves, "Don't do this. Don't do that." Such an approach cannot succeed because it relies on our own resolve and determination rather than the grace of God. It's flesh-powered Christianity.

The problem is we have been eating from the forbidden tree for so long we just don't see it. We think the remedy for bad behavior is good behavior. We think the solution for sin is to lay down the law. "Just stop it!" But this a misuse of the law. It's like fighting fire with gasoline.

The law is good but it is not your friend. We have a far better friend in Jesus.

The death he died, he died to sin once for all; but the life he lives, he lives to God. In the same way, count yourselves dead to sin but alive to God in Christ Jesus. (Romans 6:10–11)

If our co-inclusion with Christ's death is to mean anything at all, we need to consider the nature of his death. "He died to sin once for all." Sin has no claim on Jesus therefore sin has no claim on you. Sin's wage has been paid and all outstanding debts have been cancelled. You don't need to do anything to earn your freedom; you *are* free. Freedom is your starting point.

So how do we walk in that freedom? "Count yourselves dead to sin." Your old master Sin will tempt you and pester you and try and bait you back into captivity. One of Sin's more cunning strategies is to sow sinful desires into your mind and make you believe they are your desires. Do not be fooled. You have the mind of Christ and Jesus never has a sinful thought. So if a sinful thought enters your head you can rest assured it did not originate in your sound mind. Don't take ownership of it. If it flew in your left ear let it fly out your right. But what you must not do is engage with it. Don't react, don't dialogue, don't wrestle. Just play dead.

Playing dead is your best response to a provocateur such as the devil. Understand that the devil doesn't particularly care how you respond to sinful desires as long as you respond in the flesh. Sin like a sinner or resist like a Pharisee and he wins because you will be distracted from the grace that preserves you. Your eyes will be on your sinful- or self-righteous self instead of Jesus.

That's the first part; here is the second. "Reckon yourself alive to God in Christ Jesus." If all we did was play dead life would be dead dull. Life is meant to be lived in spite of all the temptations we face. We have to live for something, so let us live for him and his righteousness (1 Peter 2:24). If we react to anything, let us react to Jesus and the beauty of his holiness.

Choosing to live for Jesus is spiritual warfare. It is resisting the devil by submitting to God. It is the choice that brings ever-increasing freedom and freedom is fun!

Dealing with forbidden fruit

Let me give you an example of how this works in my own life. I am a happily married man in a world where there is ample temptation to be unfaithful to my wife. (Being tempted is not a sin. Jesus was tempted in every way yet was without sin.) If a pretty girl walks past and a tempting thought enters my head, there are two ways I can respond. The carnal way is to preach law to myself in a frenzy of grim determination. *I must not think adulterous thoughts. I must not think adulterous thoughts.* Well you can guess where that will take me. Since I am relying on my own willpower and strength, I will inevitably end up captive to sin if I fall or self-righteousness if I don't. It's a lose-lose proposition.

The spiritual way is to react to temptation with utter deadness and make no provision for the lust of the flesh. I don't gaze at the forbidden fruit but instead make a conscious decision to live for Christ. In my case this means I'll start thanking God for Camilla. I'll begin to praise him for the gift of marriage and a wife who loves me. That may not seem particularly spiritual but it is for I am consciously acknowledging my dependence on Jesus. I am recognizing him as the source of all my blessings.

But what if I wasn't married? How would I respond to temptation if I was single? In that case I might respond like this: "Thank you, Lord, for creating ladies. You did a particularly fine job with that one who just walked past. And thank you, Lord that you know me inside and out. I trust you completely. I know you will meet all my needs according to your rich supply." Again, this is the spiritual response because it is the faith response. I am choosing not to worry but to present my requests to God (Philippians 4:6). I am choosing to trust the One who knows me and my needs better than I know myself. I am choosing to run after Jesus rather than the woman.

The faith response looks like self-denial but it isn't. I am not saying "No" to my needs, I am saying "Yes" to Jesus. Big difference. Self-denial is a moral choice that offers merely moral rewards but I am motivated by the pure pleasure of right living. I am delighting myself in the Lord because he is the Lover of my soul. He, not my wife nor some strange woman on the street, is the one who gives and fulfills the deepest desires of my heart.

This revelation is the story of my life. Two roads diverged in the woods, I followed Jesus, and that has made all the difference.

What if I stumble, what if I fall?

So far, so good. But let's be realistic. Occasionally, you may forget that you are no longer Sin's slave and stumble, and when you do it's not going to be pretty. What happens then? Well, two things will happen. The accuser of the brethren will start pounding you with the crowbar of condemnation. "Look what you did! You're a terrible person. How dare you call yourself a Christian?" You shouldn't be surprised by this. If you open the door to the devil, he's going to make a mess in your house because that's what he does. But while all this is going on, the Holy Spirit will seek to convict you of your righteousness in Christ because that's what *he* does.

Again, because you are free, you have a choice. Who will you listen to? Will you listen to the Lord of Life who declares you are righteous even when you sin? Or will you listen to your old master, the Father of Lies, who says you are an unregenerate sinner? Your flesh will say, "Look at the evidence, the devil must be right." But your faith will say, "Are you kidding me?! Look to the cross and trust Jesus!"

We all stumble from time to time; it's what you do when you fall that counts. If you form a tag team with the devil and start beating yourself up, well, you're acting like your old ignorant self. But if you can find the faith to thank Jesus for loving you despite your faults, then you will rise in true repentance transformed by his grace and freer than ever before.

Walk after the flesh and you cannot win. But walk in the newness of the spirit and you cannot lose. When you walk in the revelation that your old self has died and your life is now hidden with Christ in God, Sin cannot touch you and life becomes a win-win scenario.

The gospel of your death

The gospel is not a reform program for bad people; it is the liberating declaration of new life for those who have died. The new cannot come until the old has gone and on the cross the old went. Every manmade religion preaches self-denial and dying to self. The gospel simply declares: "You died."

If anyone is in Christ, he is a new creation; the old has gone, the
new has come! (2 Corinthians 5:17)

NEW

The day I got married, I became something I had never been
before — a married man. I was single no more. The old had gone
and the new had come. Admittedly, I was a very inexperienced
married man with much to learn about his new identity. But the
thrill of marriage is learning how to be married when you are
married. It is one of life's great adventures.

Marriage gives us a good picture of how things are with us
and Jesus. When you entered into union with Christ, you literally
became a new person. The old went and the new came. Yet many
Christians don't know this. They think the old is going and the
new is still coming. They are caravanning somewhere between
Egypt and Canaan. They are striving to become who they already
are and are missing much of the thrill of being married to Jesus. It
is a heartbreaking tragedy. Instead of resting in the Promised
Land of his love, they are wandering in the wilderness of their
works.

People like this go to church and study the Bible because they
want to become a better person, pleasing to God. There is nothing
wrong with wanting to better yourself, but you have to understand that in Christ, you are already as good and pleasing to God
as you ever will be. You are not on a journey to newness; you are
already new.

If this sounds too good to be true, let me ask you two questions. What did Jesus come to give us? He came to give us new life.
Where is this new life found? It is experienced in union with Jesus:

God has given us eternal life, and this life is in his Son. He who has the Son has life; he who does not have the Son of God does not have life. (1 John 5:11b–12)

Someone who comes to Christ automatically receives his new life. This is a divine transaction, not a religious journey. It is a resuscitation, not a road trip. It is Lazarus rising from the dead. This is what happened to you. One moment you were dead in sins, and the next you were alive in Christ. Badaboom. "Lazarus, come forth!" The old has gone, the new has come. Time to start living.

The myth of the middle

As a child in Sunday school I used to think that new life was simply an extension to my current life. Instead of dying, I got to live forever. That is true but it doesn't begin to capture what is new about this new life we have in Christ.

When you got plugged into Jesus, his life began flowing through you with divine vitality. You were regenerated by the living and imperishable word of God (1 Peter 1:23). It was such a dramatic and lasting change that you instantly became a different person.

"If anyone is in Christ, he is a new creation." The word translated "new" means new in kind.[1] Anyone who is in Christ is a new kind of creature. You have not been improved or modified but wholly remade. So don't ever call yourself "a sinner saved by grace." You were a sinner; then you were saved by grace. Now you are a sinner no more. You are a new kind of person. You are a saint.

Right here is where the good news of grace parts company from the religion that many of us have grown up with. We have been told we are works in progress as if there was some middle ground between saint and sinner. There is no middle ground. You're either dead or alive, lost or found, in Christ or out of him.

Yet the in-betweeners persist with the myth of the middle saying things like, "I'm not perfect, just forgiven." Such a statement appeals to our flesh and accords with our experience but it is an insult to the One by whose sacrifice we have been made perfect forever.

"But Paul, look at me. I am a mess. I've still got plenty of faults I need to work on."

It's true that on your own you are not perfect. You are far from perfect. But that's the point. You are not on your own any longer. You have been united with the Lord, and there are no unholy branches on that holy vine.

Light and dark cannot coexist. Neither can perfection and imperfection coexist. For the Lord to have any sort of union with you, he had to make you into something you weren't and he did.

The real you

When you came to Christ, you literally became a brand-new creature. You were cleansed from sin, re-gened, and joined in vital union with the Lord. You are no longer part of Adam's race. You are a son or daughter of the Everlasting Father. Christ is your life. You stand on his faith and are cloaked in his love. Your present and passing imperfections are hidden within his eternal and sublime perfections.

When God looks at you, he doesn't just see who you are now, with your visible faults and hidden glory. He sees who you are in eternity. He sees the real you, and from his timeless perspective you are faultless, blameless, and radiant with glory.

I don't claim to be a poet, but some time ago I penned a few lines describing our new identity in Christ. The words below should be familiar to you since I stole them all from the Bible. The question for you is, do you believe them? Do you define yourself based on your imperfect performance or his finished work? Do you see yourself as a half-holy, half-righteous work in progress, or as one born to new life in the Lord?

Read the poem below through the eyes of faith. As you read it, tell yourself, "This is me; this is who I am."

Who Am I?

I am a saint, a trophy of Christ's victory
I am born again of imperishable seed
I am a new creation, complete in Christ and perfect forever
I am a child of God, the apple of my Father's eye
I am one with the Lord and the temple of the Holy Spirit

I am eternally redeemed and completely forgiven
I am seated with Christ in heavenly places
I am righteous, holy, and blameless
I am hidden in Christ and eternally secure
I am my beloved's and he is mine

I am the head and not the tail
I am blessed with every spiritual blessing, a joint heir with
    Christ
I am a competent minister of the new covenant
I am bona fide and qualified, chosen and anointed
I am his royal ambassador, a missionary to the world

I am as bold as a lion and more than a conqueror
I am the salt of the earth and the light of the world
I am the sweet smell of Jesus to those who are perishing
I am a tree planted by the water, and I am a fruitful branch
I am king o' the world because His victory is mine!

I am the disciple whom Jesus loves
And by the grace of God I am what I am.[2]

What's new?

The New Testament paints many pictures of our new life but, for me, one of the best things about it is the indwelling Holy Spirit. It was the Holy Spirit who led me to Jesus and who constantly reminds me that I am my Father's dearly beloved son.

The Holy Spirit is also the best evidence that the old has gone and the new has come. Think about it. In the old days we were separated from the life of God and strangers to his love. Surely God loved us but we didn't know his love. Now we do. How did this happen? God poured his love into our hearts by the Holy Spirit (Romans 5:5). Do you love God? Then thank the Holy Spirit who made you new.

At one time we didn't believe God existed or, if he did, we thought he was no friend of ours. But now we call him Abba Father. This is a miracle! Again, this was the Holy Spirit's doing (see Romans 8:15–16).

In the old days we dismissed the things of God as foolishness. The Bible made no sense to us. But now we find therein the words of life. We receive them with joy. Again, this is the work of the Holy Spirit. When he gives revelation the lights go on and the simple are made wise.

At one time we held no special opinion about Jesus, but now he is our greatest love and the Shepherd of our souls. That's a new thing. Before we were saved we didn't really care what other people thought about Jesus but now we do. Our heart's desire is for none to perish and all to know him. This too is a new thing.

Don't you see how much you have changed?

I will give you a new heart and put a new spirit in you. (Ezekiel 36:26a)

When the Holy Spirit came into your life the change in you was like night and day. It's like you were given a heart transplant. Your old heart, which was captive to desires of the flesh and enslaved to sin, was replaced with a new heart with new desires and appetites. Your new heart beats with new passions and they are the passions of the Holy Spirit. This is why John can say outlandish things like this:

No one who lives in him keeps on sinning. No one who continues to sin has either seen him or known him. (1 John 3:6)

Before I understood what was new about me, I used to look at verses like this sideways. *No one keeps on sinning?! John, have you lost touch with reality?* In a manner of speaking I think this is exactly what happened. John understood that there is no comparison between the life we had in Adam and the new life we now have in Christ. Sinning is characteristic of Adam's nature, not Christ's. For us, sinning is a part of that old reality that died with Christ on the cross. It does not describe our new reality in Christ.

"But Paul, are you saying we won't ever sin? Now *you're* starting to sound like you've lost touch with reality." Maybe I have. Maybe I have traded the flawed and false reality of my old life for the better and truer reality of his.

A promise, not a condition

So what is John talking about when he says no one who lives in him keeps on sinning? There are two ways to read this. Someone schooled in the sticks and carrots of the old covenant will interpret these words as a threat. "If you want to remain in him *and stay saved,* you had better stop sinning." This terrifying demand will usually be followed by a religious rant that will leave you feeling anything but new: "Don't be deceived. God is holy and intolerant of sin. Slip up once and you're outta here!"

What an awful distortion of God's unconditional love. Can you imagine being married to someone who threatened to kick you out every time you made a mistake? You would be an emotional wreck. You would walk on eggshells for fear of upsetting your hyper-sensitive and ungracious partner.

Come to think of it, this is exactly how many Christians live. Since they are not aware of the grace that both saves and keeps them, they are filled with performance anxiety. They are ever fearful of enraging a temperamental God.

Look to the cross! If God loved you enough to die for you when you were a sinner, he surely loves you now. He didn't stop loving you after you got saved and he will never kick you out. Your union with the Lord is not conditional on your behavior. In case we had forgotten this, John gives us a timely reminder:

Whoever confesses that Jesus is the Son of God, God abides in him, and he in God. (1 John 4:15, NKJV)

John says he *abides*, he *dwells*, he *stays*. The moment you acknow-
ledged Jesus as Lord — literally, the saving Son of God — he moved
into your life and he will never leave. How do we know? How can
we be sure he will stay given there are so many grim preachers
making threats? Because he promised:

> For he [God] Himself has said, I will not in any way fail
> you nor give you up nor leave you without support. I will
> not, I will not, I will not in any degree leave you helpless
> nor forsake nor let you down (relax My hold on you)!
> Assuredly not! (Hebrews 13:5b, AMP)

John's remarks about not sinning should not be read as a
threat but a promise. He is describing the new reality of the life we
have in Christ. Jesus didn't sin and he never will. If you let him
live his life through you, then without any conscious effort on
your part you're going to start talking and walking just like sinless
Jesus. It's inevitable. Live with someone long enough and you
begin to resemble that person in manner and thought.

I am not saying your behavior will attain a level of sinless perfection this side of eternity. I am saying that living in fellowship
with the sinless Son produces desires in us that are informed by
his righteous nature. You are Sonful not sinful.

This is how John explains it:

> No one who is *born of God* will continue to sin, because
> *God's seed remains* in him; he cannot go on sinning, because
> he has been *born of God*. (1 John 3:9)

This is not about your performance but your pedigree. Look at
the verse again. Three times John refers to your parentage; *born of
God, God's seed, born of God*.

John is trying to tell us that while Adam breeds sinners, God
does not. This point comes out clearly in the Message Bible:

> People conceived and brought into life by God don't make
> a practice of sin. How could they? God's seed is deep
> within them, making them who they are. It's not in the

118

nature of the God-begotten to practice and parade sin. (1 John 3:9, The Message)

Origin determines destination. In your old life you followed in the faithless footsteps of your father Adam. You walked after the desires of the flesh because they were the only desires you had. But you have been taken out of Adam and placed into Christ. You have become a partaker of his divine nature. The evidence of this is the new desires and new ambitions you now have. As far as sinning goes, you are just not that interested anymore. Sure, you still have the capacity to sin. But you don't enjoy it like you used to. Sinning makes you miserable because you know who your Father is, and when you know who your Father is (not a sinner), then you begin to know who you are (not a sinner).

In the next verse John adds, "This is how we know who the children of God are" (1 John 3:10). Who are the children of God? It is those who practice righteousness, not because they have to, but because they carry the righteous DNA of their righteous Father. You don't practice righteousness to become righteous but because you are righteous. You are a righteous branch on a righteous vine doing what comes naturally.

No liars in heaven

With our new identity securely grounded in our union with Christ, we can begin to understand why the Bible draws big fat lines between who we are and who we used to be:

Do you not know that the wicked will not inherit the kingdom of God? Do not be deceived: Neither the sexually immoral nor idolaters nor adulterers nor male prostitutes nor homosexual offenders nor thieves nor the greedy nor drunkards nor slanderers nor swindlers will inherit the kingdom of God. (1 Corinthians 6:9–10)

This sounds like God hates slanderers and swindlers. He doesn't. He loves slanderers and swindlers! When Jesus walked the earth, he spent time with slanderers and swindlers.[3] However, slanderers and swindlers will not inherit the kingdom of God. Indeed, they cannot. Why not? Because slanderers and swindlers who come to Jesus don't remain slanderers and swindlers. They become new. A good thing that is too, otherwise the kingdom of heaven would be empty.

> But the cowardly, the unbelieving, the vile, the murderers, the sexually immoral, those who practice magic arts, the idolaters and all liars — their place will be in the fiery lake of burning sulfur. This is the second death. (Revelation 21:8)

God has high standards — no liars admitted. And indeed, there are no liars in the kingdom, only former liars who have been made new. Neither are there any fornicators in the kingdom, only former fornicators who have been made new. (Do you see it yet?) This is why the good news is good. The good news is the happy announcement that God is in the business of turning old, damaged people into new, holy people. He turns slanderers and swindlers into saints and sons.

If this is too much to swallow in one go, take a detour to the Bible's own Hall of Fame in Hebrews 11. Here you will find a list of Old Testament men and women who were all commended for their faith. These guys were so impressive their names got recorded in *both* testaments. Who are these heroes, these figures of renown? Well there's Noah (a one-time drunk), Abraham (he slept with the maid), and Jacob (a swindler if ever there was one). There is also a murderer (Moses), a prostitute (Rahab), and a double-dealing king (David).

David, as you know, got another man's wife pregnant and then had that man killed to cover up his crime. So what does that make David? In the eyes of the law he is condemned as an adulterer and a murderer. Such a man will not inherit the kingdom of God; the Bible says so. And yet I am certain we will meet David in eternity. How do I know? Because David trusted in the One who makes all things new. In God's eyes, David is not a sinner but a son and a co-heir with Christ. So am I. So are you.

Learning to walk

There is a world of difference between a sinner who sins and a saint who sins. Finding sins on a sinner is like finding lemons on a lemon tree. It's no big surprise. But a saint who sins is like a rich man stealing coins from parking meters. It's not something you expect to see. At least that's the theory. In practice sinning saints are fairly common. But the reason some saints continue to act like old sinners is not because there is something defective about the new life they have been given. It is because they have not yet learned to walk in the newness of their new life. They've got the car but they haven't learned how to drive.

> Therefore we were buried with him through baptism into death, that just as Christ was raised from the dead by the glory of the Father, even so we also should walk in newness of life. (Romans 6:4, NKJV)

When you received the life of Christ and were made new, the change was instantaneous. To use an old metaphor, it's like you were born again. And like a newborn you have to learn how to walk. No one comes walking out of the womb on brand-new legs.

Learning to walk takes time. It's not easy at first and you may stumble and fall. When that happens an old covenant preacher will point to your failings and say, "There, you see? Your falls prove you are still an old sinner by nature. Nothing's changed. You had better ask God to crucify you afresh. Life's a struggle. Next time try harder." Heed this advice and the prophecy will become self-fulfilling. Your life will indeed be a struggle because you are trying to walk in your own strength. You will wear yourself out going nowhere fast and you will end up a miserable advertisement for Jesus.

But listen to the new covenant preacher and you will hear a completely different message. "Christ is your life. You can do all things through him who strengthens you. Now fix your eyes on him and walk, baby walk!"

You may say, "But what about all these sins I'm still dealing with?" And the new covenant preacher will remind you of Jesus our advocate, who defends us, and Jesus our high priest, who deals gently with those going astray.[4] Then, after giving you an assurance of your secure position in Christ, the new covenant preacher will encourage you to, "Set your mind on things above, not on earthly things. Put off the old self (it's dead) and put on the new (it's who you are)."

I'm paraphrasing the New Testament here because I want you to see that the epistles are full of encouraging exhortations for saints who are learning how to walk. "Gird up the loins of your mind." "Walk in the light." "Walk as Jesus did."[5] These exhortations should not be read as commands to be obeyed as though God was judging our walking performance. What kind of Father faults his children for stumbling when they are learning to walk? Rather, they should be received as Daddy's words of loving encouragement as we take our first steps into the new life he has given us. God is for you! He and that great cloud of witnesses are cheering you on!

Christianity is Christ

Of course there is much more to this new life than "not sinning," just as there is more to marriage than "not being single." We are not defined by who *we used to be* but by *who Jesus is*. "As he is, so are we in this world" (1 John 4:17). Boom! So much for the idea that there are levels to Christianity and that you have to work your way up to Christ-likeness. His supernatural life is not something you achieve; it's something you receive.

Christianity is Christ; nothing more, nothing less. We need to define life through the unfiltered lens of Jesus. He is not our role model; *he is our life*. He is in you and he wants out. He has a hand to play and, guess what, it's your hand.

Jesus said anyone who believes in him would do the works he did and greater works besides (John 14:12). This comment usually sparks an incredulous response. "Have you seen the sorts of things Jesus did? And we're supposed to top that?! I just can't see that happening." Either Jesus was fibbing or we don't believe what he says about us. I'm not saying we consciously reject the truth. It's just that we haven't learned to walk in it. So learn. Ask

God to give you the Spirit of wisdom and revelation so that you may know him better, and so that you may begin to understand every good thing that is in you in Christ Jesus.[6]

Learning to walk in the newness of life can be scary but the Holy Spirit is a wonderful teacher. He knows exactly how to coach us and he is so gentle. He never scolds us but patiently encourages us to be the new people we already are. As we learn to trust him, we discover that walking in the newness of life is quite simply the most thrilling occupation there is.

The gospel of new life

The cross is good but the resurrection's better. The reason we died with him was so that we might live with him — not fifty years hence, not in the hereafter, but here and now. Eternal life is the sheer adventure of knowing and experiencing God today. It is dancing on the grave of our self-centeredness and enjoying the abundant life of the Spirit. It is saying goodbye to sin and hello to righteousness. It is revealing his supernatural life to those we live, work, and play with. It's a whole new way of life for a whole new kind of people.

The gospel is not a half-baked hope that you can extend your old, broken life indefinitely. The gospel is the joyful announcement that in Christ the old has gone and the new has come.

You are a chosen people, a royal priesthood, a holy nation ...
(1 Peter 2:9)

R O Y A L

I once passed the small hours of the night having drinks with a prince of a European nation. It was one of those accidental encounters life dishes out from time to time. A friend said he was going to meet someone and asked if I would like to tag along. I went and learned that the person we were going to meet was second in line to his country's throne. At first I was a bit starstruck, but the young prince turned out to be a fairly ordinary bloke. We chatted for hours.

One thing that was confirmed to me as a result of that experience is that royalty is not what it used to be. I saw none of the historic trappings of nobility. There was no carriage, no scepter, and no crown. Today, few European monarchs have any real power or authority. If you were to pass them in the street you would not recognize them for who they really are. The same could be said of most Christians.

Peter said we are "a chosen people, a royal priesthood and a holy nation" but what did he mean? Peter's words roll off our tongues like lines we learned in school, but do we really understand what we are saying? Let's find out.

Do you believe that you are chosen, holy, and royal? If you have made it this far through the book hopefully you will say yes to at least two of those three adjectives. But for many people, these are just words. They do not see themselves as favored, which is what chosen means. Neither do they consider themselves as particularly holy. And as for royal, well that's just not an adjective most would use to describe themselves.

But royal you are—Peter says so—and not in a distant "I'm married to the third cousin of the Queen's sister" sort of way. You are wedded to the King of kings. You are royalty indeed.

> And [Jesus] did make us kings and priests to his God and Father ... (Revelation 1:6, YLT)

You were a slave but Jesus made you into a king and a priest. That's quite a turnaround and I can understand if you are a little unsettled by the idea. Perhaps you are more comfortable with your priestly role than your kingly role. Depending on your denominational background, you will be at least somewhat open to the idea that every Christian is a minister.[1] But the Bible also declares that every Christian is also a king. We are not merely a kingdom of priests, we are king-priests. Or priest-kings. (Take your pick.) We are called to serve in a priestly capacity and rule in a kingly capacity.

> And You have made them a kingdom (royal race) and priests to our God, and they shall reign [as kings] over the earth! (Revelation 5:10, AMP)

"Ah yes, Paul. That's for later, not now. We are kings in training. We won't actually rule anything until Jesus returns." Well by that logic you are not a real priest because the two go together. He has made us "kings and priests." You are not one or the other but both.

Blue-blooded believers

Heaven regards us as kings because our Father is kingly. Your born-again blood runs royal blue. Yes, there is a training aspect involved and we won't see the fullness of our kingly roles until Jesus returns. But it ill befits the children of a king to act like commoners or slaves. We have a God-given mandate to rule and reign here and now. This has been God's plan from the beginning:

Then God said, "Let us make man in our image, in our likeness, and let them rule ..." (Genesis 1:26)

You were born to rule. You are called to be the head and not the tail. The Hebrew word for rule means to tread down and subjugate.[2] Such a strong word should leave us in no doubt regarding God's intentions. When he told Adam to "fill the earth and subdue it," he wasn't inviting our forefather to trash the planet. He was saying, "This is your home. You're in charge. Take care of it" (see Genesis 1:28).

Adam was given a king's authority over the earth and the animals but his reign was short-lived. Two chapters later he gave his authority to a usurper disguised as one of the very animals he was supposed to rule. But God's plan has not changed. Just as Adam was to rule in the name of God, we are to rule in the name of his Son. Every Christian has a royal calling to reveal Christ the King and the glad tidings of his kingdom.

God makes kings

God told Abraham he would be "the father of many nations and kings will come from you."[3] Abraham's offspring—the children of the faith—are meant to be kings.

Kingship has to do with authority and power. Adam was given authority over the earth and lost it to Satan. We know this because of what the devil said when he showed Jesus all the kingdoms of the world: "All their authority and splendor has been given to me" (see Luke 4:6). But last Adam took back what the devil stole and before he ascended into heaven, he revealed his kingly glory: "All authority in heaven and on earth has been given to me" (Matthew 28:18).

The war has been fought and won and the devil is defeated. Yet many of his works are still with us. As believers our role is to represent the Victor and his victory in those areas that remain under the influence of darkness. We are to fill the earth with the knowledge of his glory by ruling over sickness, demonic spirits, and all the works of the enemy.[4]

In our union with Christ Jesus he raised us up with him to rule with him in the heavenly world. (Ephesians 2:6, GNB)

This leads to some sobering questions: Why do bad things happen to good people? Why do people get sick and die prematurely? Why do the innocent suffer? Theologians blame sin, followers of Job blame a sovereign God, but look at what the Bible says:

The highest heavens belong to the Lord, but the earth he has given to man. (Psalms 115:16)

This planet is our responsibility. It was given to us and we were told to rule it. Why do bad things happen? It is because we—the kings called to rule in God's name—allow them to happen. It was *one of us* who gave the planet to Satan, and it was Jesus acting as *one of us* who took it back. When you think about it, the history of the world has our fingerprints all over it. We have far more say in what goes on than we give ourselves credit for.

The problem is not that we lack authority like a European prince. The problem is that we don't walk in the authority God has given us. Perhaps we think we are too young or too old or we don't have enough training or we need more anointing. Perhaps we are just sitting idly by waiting for Jesus to return. Whatever our excuse, the outcome is the same. When we abdicate our kingly role people suffer. Consider Adam. A treacherous enemy slithered into his realm, Adam did nothing, and humanity ended up on death row. Bad things happen because kings do nothing to stop them.

When industries collapse and companies fold, it's easy to point the finger at corporate fat cats and sleeping watchdogs. But spoilers and slackers have always been with us and playing the blame game solves nothing. A better question to ask is, where were we? Where were the kings who rule with wisdom and justice? Unbelief thrives in a culture of victimhood but faith brings the victory that overcomes the world (see 1 John 5:4). Passive unbelief stays on the sidelines and doesn't lift a finger to help, but faith raises its hand — it volunteers, it speaks out, it defends and seeks to administer justice in the name of a righteous king.

The heart of the Great King

True kings rule. They draw lines in the sand and say, "This far and no further." They protect and bless those around them and take ownership of other people's problems. Jesus is a prime example. He didn't have to leave the comforts of heaven and die for us but he did. This was a noble and kingly act. He saw our sorry state and said, "I am going to come and tread upon their problem even if it kills me."

The heart of this Great King beats in your heart. His Spirit is one with your spirit. Jesus didn't hang up his crown after ascending to heaven. He plans to reign until all his enemies have been defeated. Through your union with Christ, you are destined to reign.

> For if, by the trespass of the one man, death reigned through that one man, how much more will those who receive God's abundant provision of grace and of the gift of righteousness reign in life through the one man, Jesus Christ. (Romans 5:17)

Adam's failure to be a king condemned the human race. His sin opened the door to death, disease, defeat, discouragement, and disappointment. But we who were victims of Adam's disobedience have become victorious through Christ's obedience.

There is a new king in town and his name is Grace. Under Adam death reigned, but under Grace *we* reign. However, not every Christian *does* reign. Many are racked with guilt and tortured by condemnation. They struggle with sin and live in fearful anxiety. Problems assail them from every side and they are unsuccessful in much of what they do. Although Christ has provided all we need for the abundant life of royalty, they are not enjoying it. They are the paupers in the palace.

Why do some live like this? This isn't rocket science. If there is little evidence of the grace of God in your life that doesn't mean

God is tightfisted. Far from it. It means you have not received from his abundant provision of grace. The incalculable riches of grace have been deposited into your account but you have not made any withdrawals. I don't say this to belittle your faith but to recognize that most of us have been raised in a culture of unbelief.

We are constantly hearing that God has *not* provided all we need to rule and reign, and that there are things *we* must do to make that happen. This faithless message is loudest in the church that does not walk in grace. Ironically, this is exactly the sort of church where you will often hear that you must live by faith, pray with faith, and walk by faith, as if talking about faith had the power to magically make things happen. The trouble is nothing ever does happen and when *that* happens you'll be told you didn't have enough faith. "You gotta have more faith and here is a list of things you have to do to get it."

Walking by faith is walking in grace. There is no difference. If you would walk by faith, learn to walk in his grace. Learn to receive what He has already provided. Stop begging him to act and start thanking him for what he's done.

Beware cheap grace?

Only those who receive from God's abundant provision of grace get to reign in life. One thing that can stop us from receiving is the lie that says we have to prove our mettle before God will bless us; we have to get cleaned up, straightened out, and dried out before we can receive. This is a grace-killing doctrine of demons. It's like telling sick people they have to get well before the doctor will see them.

Every blessing there is, whether health, deliverance, provision, or salvation, comes to us by grace and grace alone. To think we must work for the blessings of God is to try and buy that which is not for sale.

Those who don't get this worry that those who do are pushing cheap grace. They fret that we are giving away the treasures of heaven without first requiring people to turn from sin, get baptized, confess, and do all the other things that supposedly describe the cost of discipleship. They don't understand that grace comes first, that it is only by grace that we can forgive the unforgivable, love the unlovable, and do all the other things that followers of Christ do.

Beware cheap grace? There is no such thing. Grace is free or it's not grace. Or rather grace is priceless and you can't afford it.

There is simply nothing you can do to earn the Lord's acceptance and favor. If you are wondering why God is not pleased with your sacrifices, maybe it's because you are not pleased with his.

I have personally encountered hundreds of people who are confused by the good news of God's grace. When I explain it in simple terms, as I have just done, some of them come back to me with qualifiers and caveats and long lists of reasons outlining why I am wrong. They may respond fifty different ways but behind it all is a heart of unbelief. "It just can't be that simple. Grace can't be free. There must be a price to pay." There is and Jesus paid it.

If I am wrong about grace then one day I will have to apologize to God for telling everyone he is better and more gracious than he really is. But if the grace killers are wrong, then eternity for them is going to begin with a truly awkward moment. "Er, sorry Lord. Sorry for prostituting your love and making people pay for the free gift of grace."

Standing with the schmucks

Every single Christian thinks he or she has a handle on grace, even the ones who don't. But the proof of the pudding is whether they have received the gift of righteousness. Paul said those who receive grace and righteousness reign in life. The test of a king — your sword in the stone, if you like — is whether you have taken hold of his righteousness. If you don't receive it you won't reign. Instead you will toil like Adam and curse what God has blessed. Even though you are free in Christ, you won't live free. You will bear the heavy yoke of manmade religion and become easy prey for the spirit of intimidation. You will come under the demonic control of others. Something like this happened in Peter's life.

Along with Paul, Peter had a revelation that Christ died for all people and not just the Jews. This revelation changed him. As he allowed the heart of Christ to be revealed in his own life, Peter began to accept Gentiles even to the point of eating with them.

However, when certain men from James came to Antioch, Peter drew back from the Gentiles in fear. He separated himself because he was unsure of his righteousness. "Am I right? Maybe I'm not. Those Judaizers look the business. They've got titles. They've got theology and a list of scriptures explaining why I am wrong. I had better listen to them." Instead of standing up for the Gentiles like a king, Peter stood with the critics like a schmuck and Paul rebuked him for it (see Galatians 2:11-13).

The strange thing about Peter's behavior is that he should have known better. God accepts people from every nation and Peter knew this. God had given him a dramatic rooftop vision featuring animals and sheets that somehow made everything clear (see Acts 10:9-28). But when push came to shove, Peter abdicated his kingly role and took himself out of the game. He feared those of the circumcision group because they were more confident of their self-righteousness than he was of his righteousness in Christ Jesus.

Kings are confident and that confidence comes from knowing you are righteous. When you know that God is for you—that he loves you, accepts you, and is well pleased with you—it changes everything. You no longer hang back on the fringes of the kingdom like a fraud and you no longer tolerate the grace-killing lies of religion. You begin to reign. You begin to walk and talk like a child of the Most High. You begin to live out your destiny.

You don't need to go to King School to become a king. You just need to see yourself as your Father sees you. You need to receive in your heart what he has said, act on it, and leave the results to him.

The gospel declares that in him you are righteous. As you walk in this revelation, your confidence will grow and you will start to exercise your kingly influence. You will pray less like a beggar and more like a commander. If someone in your family gets sick, something inside of you will respond, "Not on my watch." You will rebuke the sickness and appropriate by faith the healing that Jesus paid for. And after you have seen one or two get healed—after you have killed your lion and your bear—you will have the confidence to start gunning for the giants that terrorize your land. Then you will be a king indeed.

King-sized exploits

Kings are problem solvers. They see giants and snakes, sickness and sin, and all the other ills of the world as problems to tread upon and overcome. They understand that for every earthly problem there is a heavenly solution. Kings are not intimidated by the size of their problem because they have seen the size of their God.

Kings don't claim to have all the answers; they just know where to find them. They possess a 24 hour access pass to the throne of grace where they can go for help in their hour of need (see Hebrews 4:16). Holding fast to the gift of his righteousness, these kings do not hesitate to come boldly in and make their requests known to God.

Common folk live within the limits of the natural realm but kings operate in a higher reality. They have an abiding sense that while we may be losing sleep over our present needs, God is not. "He's not trying to figure out what to do. He already knows."

Problems that stump ordinary men drive kings to pray. "Lord, I don't know the way to go but you do. Please show me the way." It is the glory of kings to search out a matter and they do this principally by asking for wisdom and inspiration. Like King Jehoshaphat, they respond to the fog of uncertainty by praying, "Lord, we do not know what to do, but our eyes are upon you" (see 2 Chronicles 20:12).

Kings bless those around them by releasing the resources of heaven in response to earthly needs. At one level they confront the destructive works of the devil by liberating the poor and needy, the sick and oppressed. But kings also exercise influence by taking people places no one has ever been. Through creative expression in the arts, sciences, business, and politics, kings bring the culture of heaven to earth.

Kings are unafraid to try new things and generally excel at all they do. It is no coincidence that Israel's greatest kings were also gifted soldiers, poets, musicians, and administrators. Those who are accustomed to drawing on the manifold wisdom of the Lord typically experience success in a range of fields. Not content to be pigeonholed, kings make a habit of stepping out into new ventures knowing that God has promised to bless *all* the work of their hands (Deuteronomy 28:12).

> The people that do know their God shall be strong, and do exploits. (Daniel 11:32b, KJV)

Kings get their kicks by releasing the power of God into situations that defy human management. It's not that they are opposed to the means of men, it's just that flesh-based solutions strike them as inferior and slow. "You've suffered with this problem for how long?! God can fix this right now!" Kings find natural limits restrictive and stifling. They would much rather co-labor with the Lord and bring glory to his name by doing the impossible thing. Total dependence on the Lord is a king's greatest strength and the secret to his success.

In the natural the kings of his kingdom may appear to be normal people. They may not look like much yet they live king-sized lives and do king-sized exploits. They routinely alter the course of history for individuals and families, companies and cities. Kings disciple nations.

The show and tell gospel

The grace of God is better than we think. Not only does it turn sinners into saints and make dead men live, it is able to restore relationships, transform communities, and bless entire countries. It is my conviction that as more people begin to walk in the kingly ways of his grace, we will discover that God really is able to do exceedingly more than we ask or imagine. We may be waiting for God to act but a poor and needy world is waiting for us, his kings and priests, to release through faith the royal riches of his kingdom.

Whether you are a housewife or a president, the primary way in which you act as a king is by revealing the gospel of the kingdom. This does not mean taking to the pulpit with a three point sermon followed by an altar call. (Although if that's your thing, go for it.) Jesus revealed the good news of the kingdom simply by being himself. At synagogues, weddings, and lakeside picnics, wherever Jesus went the kingdom went. Freedom, healing, joy, and deliverance followed in his wake.

To reveal the good news of the kingdom requires that you do nothing more than reveal Jesus. The King is inseparable from his kingdom. Bring the Lord of Life to bear on whatever problem you are facing and you will inevitably release grace—the supernatural, history-changing influence of the Holy Spirit.

The gospel of the kingdom is a show and tell gospel. Jesus told people good things about their God and then he delivered them from their problems. He drove out demons with a word. He healed the sick and raised the dead. He spoke to storms and confounded the so-called wisdom of those who opposed him.

What Jesus did his disciples also did and what they did you can do too. The same Spirit that helped them helps you. So how do we start?

The word of the king

Grace comes through faith and faith must be acted upon if it is to be of any benefit. The easiest way to express faith is to speak it. Words are powerful. Words can be used to build up or tear down, guide or misdirect, clarify or confuse. The right word spoken at the right time can change the world.

Kings exercise dominion primarily by speaking. To paraphrase Ecclesiastes 8:4, "the word of the king has power." When God's kings speak God's words, God backs it up with power. This is not to glorify the word spoken in faith but to draw attention to the Living Word who lives within you. When you reveal Jesus, your words are supernaturally empowered to bring salvation to the lost and freedom to the captives. You can drive out demons and heal the sick just as he did. In fact, Jesus promised that those who believe in him would do exactly these sorts of things (Mark 16:17–18).

You may think, "But that's not how things are done where I live. I've never experienced the supernatural." But you have. God called you out of darkness and you came. Have you ever stopped to think about that? When you responded to the gospel, a miracle took place. The actual words you heard may have come from the mouth of an evangelist or a friend but the Spirit of God spoke into your heart, called you out, and you responded. Don't you see? You are living proof that word of the king has power. The gospel works; but only when it's told.

> But how can people call for help if they don't know who to trust? And how can they know who to trust if they haven't heard of the One who can be trusted? And how can they hear if nobody tells them? (Romans 10:14, The Message)

Not everyone I talk to believes the gospel, but more people believe and are set free when I talk than when I stay silent. If you are believing for the salvation and healing of your friends but your faith doesn't cause you to say or do anything, it is useless faith. I don't say this to condemn you. I want to inspire you. You are a king and your words have power; so speak them.

As kings we can command blessing where there is curse, healing where there is sickness, and life where there is death. In view of this, why would you choose to stay silent?

Do you know why Adam lost his crown in the garden? He didn't speak. The king's word has power but King Adam was speechless. He listened when he should have spoken. This is a fatal mistake for a king. Don't let the devil spew his lies over your life. Jesus didn't. When the devil challenged him in the wilderness, Jesus spoke back. I doubt anyone received the attention from the devil that Jesus did. Yet three short sentences from the Great King were enough to silence that old snake.

David is another good example of a king who spoke. Along with the rest of the Israelites, he heard the giant's intimidating taunts. But while his countrymen ran in fear, David spoke back. He rebuked the giant in the name of the Lord and prophesied his downfall. He was just a boy but David had the heart of king. He spoke from a higher reality and so became a conqueror.

You can opt out (but why would you?)

The anticipation of a future coronation precludes many believers from ruling and reigning now. They think, "One day I will be crowned but not yet. I am not a king. I am merely a humble servant in the courts of the Lord." Why are you standing in the courts when you could be seated in the throne room? This sort of servant talk appeals to our religious pride but it is an abdication of our true calling which is to be a priest-king.

You may say, "But I don't know what a priest-king looks like. I have never heard of one before." Sure you have. Did you know the first priest mentioned in the Bible was also a king? It was Melchizedek, "*king* of Salem and *priest* of God Most High" (Hebrews 7:1). And what kind of king is Jesus? He is a priest-king, in the order of Melchizedek (Hebrews 5:6). In other words, Jesus wears two hats. He is a priest who serves and a king who rules.

A servant's heart is appropriate for a priest, but a priest who is not also a king will be powerless to deal with giant-sized problems. A crownless priest will present an emasculated image of Christ. His gospel will be weak and his kingdom will be all talk.

Jesus is the servant-hearted king who served man by subduing the enemy. His disciples did the same and as we allow him to express his kingly life through us so will we.

Perhaps you are a bit awed by all this talk of slaying giants and healing the sick. Perhaps you are worried that you may fail the king test and leave the sword in the stone. Don't panic. If you run instead of rule God won't reject you. Even David ran.

In truth, there will be times when ruling and reigning seems a most unreasonable thing to do. It's not an easy thing to believe for healing when three doctors and two specialists have given a negative report. And the sight of wheelchairs at the altar call may tempt even experienced ministers to turn away and look for softer targets.[5]

We celebrate David's heroics but no one would have thought ill of him if he had fled from the lion, the bear, and the giant. Indeed, he would have been applauded for doing the smart thing. "Why fight a lion over a few dumb sheep? David, you could have died!"

If you run from the lion or the bear no one will think the less of you. You will appear to be a very sensible, lion-avoiding person, and God will still love you.

But here's the thing. *Why would you want to?*

If your child is sick or your spouse is being attacked by depression, why would you choose to stand by and do nothing? The point is not that you *have* to be a king but that you *get* to be a king. The same Spirit that enabled David to slay lions and giants empowers you to rule and reign. You have options the unbeliever lacks. You have the Holy Spirit. Given this phenomenal advantage, why would you choose to act like a mere man or woman? It makes as much sense as Superman riding the bus.

In the Bible there were two men whose families were savagely attacked by bandits. One of those men tore his clothes, sat down in the ash heap, and threw himself a pity party. The other man encouraged himself in the Lord, then hunted down and subdued his enemies. Guess which of these two men went on to become Israel's greatest king? Job was a superstitious, sacrifice-bringing navel gazer, but David was a priest-king and a man after God's own heart.[6]

The good news is that in Christ you are too.

The gospel of the kingdom

Some people treat Christianity like a game of checkers. If you live carefully and navigate your way safely to the other side you can declare "King me!" But in truth, you were kinged at the beginning of the game. The moment you were put in Christ, you became royalty.

If you have received from the abundant provision of his grace and righteousness, then you are destined to reign in life. As you walk in your kingly identity your problems will discover that in you they have more than met their match. They may be big but your God is bigger still and those who know him shall be strong and do exploits.

The gospel of the kingdom is the happy announcement that a Great King sits on the throne and his desire is to see God's will done on earth as it is in heaven. In heaven there is no sickness, no sorrow, or poverty. What is true there is his plan for here.

The gospel is not a vague notion that you get to rule and reign after you die; it is the glorious announcement that the reign of the King is right here within the reach of faith. The kingdom of God is at hand.

THE TEST OF YOUR GOSPEL

When I first went to Hong Kong in the late 1980s, an eager man on Nathan Road approached me. "You wanna buy a Rolex?" I didn't particularly want to buy a Rolex but when the watch seller named his price, I was intrigued. Fresh off the plane and I had stumbled on the bargain of a century!

Of course these weren't real Rolex watches he was selling—I knew that. But these "copy-watches" looked good enough to wear. It was only after I had handed over my cash that I began to discover just how feeble these counterfeits were. "Oh look, the hour hand goes backwards."

Like others who have lived in Asia for many years, I have become something of an expert in counterfeit goods. I have learned that while counterfeits may look like the real deal they seldom work as they are supposed to: the pirated movie is shot all out of focus; the fake handbag dissolves in the rain; the luxury pen is an ink explosion waiting to happen.

It's the same story with counterfeit gospels. They look like the real gospel but they don't actually work. They don't set you free, they don't bring lasting peace, and any joy that comes with them soon runs out.

Buy into a counterfeit gospel and it won't be long before you find yourself burdened with doubt, debt, duty, and depression. You'll discover that what you thought was good news is actually bad news sold with a fake label.

How do you recognize a counterfeit gospel? It's the one with the price tag. It's the one that makes you pay for what God has freely given. It's the gospel that treats people as prospects and demands the poor give to the rich. It's the gospel with poison in the well and fishhooks in the love.

The counterfeit gospel

The vast majority of Christians have been sold a counterfeit gospel. They have bought into a message that looks like the real thing but is demonstrably inferior.[1]

In the past few years I have met many believers who are trying to earn what God has freely given them. If you were to ask these people about grace they would declare, "Yes, I am saved by grace. I thank God for his grace." But by their works they testify that God's grace is not enough. Grace may have got them started, but now it's up to them to finish. Having begun with the Spirit they are trying to attain their goal by human effort (Galatians 3:3). Instead of working out what it means to *be saved*, they are working hard to *stay saved*.

A counterfeit gospel is what you have when someone tells you God won't accept you or bless you unless you first do something for him. Walk down the Nathan Road of manmade religion and you will be told that for a reasonable price you can become holy, righteous, and pleasing to God. "Just confess and you'll be forgiven. Just turn from sin and you'll be accepted."

Browse the shop windows of carnal Christianity and you will find dead works dressed up with respectable labels like responsibility, good works, mission, self control, sowing, and investing. I am not against these things. What I am opposed to is the lie that says God's favor depends on you and me doing them.

Make no mistake; if you think you can do anything to improve your standing with God, you are saying "Christ died for nothing" (Galatians 2:21). You are, in effect, calling Jesus a liar ("It is *not* finished") and elevating yourself to co-savior ("Jesus needs my help").

Just as fake Rolexes are sold to tourists and not locals, counterfeit gospels are sold to Christians and not sinners. Sinners get the real stuff, pure grace straight from the tap. But Christians get the dirty grace that spews from the toxic pipes of rule-based tradition. Sinners are given the unconditional love of God but Christians are made to pay for it.

A mother of four who had grown up as a pastor's kid sent me the following message after reading one of my articles on grace:

I was raised in church and I never felt like the good news of God's grace was for me. It was always for the worst kind of sinner — the one in need of God's pitying grace — and not for those of us raised inside the faith. We were expected to just behave and not touch this "cheap grace." Thanks for telling us that Gods grace is for *all*, including me. Yay!

I get messages like this all the time. They come from long-term Christians who are surprised to learn that grace is for everyone, not just sinners. It's obvious when you see it but many don't see it. Their minds are blanketed by the fog of religion. They only see the love of God through the distorted lens of performance-based Christianity.

The child test

I never meant to write such a big book. When I began, my goal was to present the authentic gospel without all the baggage that normally comes with it. It was going to be short and sweet. But, as often happens when I get talking about Jesus, I got carried away. Beginning each chapter was like walking into a room full of treasure and being told I could have whatever I could carry. The hard part was not deciding what to put in but what to leave out.

So the book turned out longer than planned. But do you really mind? Did I give you too much treasure?

Despite the length of the book, I maintain that the gospel is simple enough for a child to understand: God loves you. Period. That's it. Bow your heads and musicians to the front because I am done preaching. I'm serious — it really is that simple. *God loves you.* We will spend eternity unpacking those three little words and exploring the immeasurable reaches of his love. This is what we were born for.

I tell you the truth, anyone who will not receive the kingdom of God like a little child will never enter it. (Mark 10:15)

The gospel is so simple that a child-like understanding is required to see it. It is so uncomplicated that it confounds the wise.

Any gospel that doesn't pass the child test is no gospel at all. If you want to know whether the message you have bought into is the authentic gospel, tell it to a child. Their eyes should light up. But if you don't have a child handy, here is a simple test to reveal whether the gospel you are listening to is the same gospel Jesus revealed and Paul preached. Just ask yourself the following four questions:

1. Does this gospel cause me to fix my eyes exclusively on Jesus?

Does the message I'm hearing focus on me or does it cause me to fix my eyes on the author and perfecter of my faith? Does it emphasize what I'm doing or not doing, or does it emphasize what Christ has done? Does it make me self-conscious and introspective or Christ-conscious and grateful?

A counterfeit gospel will always put the focus on you and your effort. It will leave you thinking, "*I* have to pray, *I* have to fast, *I* have to give." The problem is not with *what* you are doing, but *why* you are doing it. What is your motive? Are you motivated by the fear of punishment or the need to deal with guilt? Are you striving to make a good impression or earn a blessing? Motive is everything.

Sometimes religion is subtle. It will tell you what you must do without clearly explaining why you should do it. Like a manipulative salesperson it will try and sell you something without showing you the price tag. Only later do you learn the true cost.

Remember, grace has no price tag. Everything in the kingdom comes to us on account of the riches of his grace alone. What you do or don't do has absolutely no bearing on this except that you can frustrate the grace of God by trying to pay for it.

A true gospel preacher will always seek to reveal more and more of Jesus. Jesus is the supreme manifestation of the character and purpose of God. He is grace personified. Any message that doesn't reveal Jesus will likely be a powerless substitute, a flesh-trip, and a wasted opportunity. Jesus is peerless and nothing compares to him. He is our wisdom from God and I will boast of nothing else (1 Corinthians 1:30–31).

Here's the test: The true gospel will lead you to trust in the all-sufficiency of Christ. It will inspire you to believe in his name — to step out, to take risks, and to act. In contrast, a counterfeit gospel promotes activity in your own name, which is a form of unbelief. The true gospel will make you increasingly dependent on Christ's love but a counterfeit gospel glorifies the flesh — your willpower, your own resources, and understanding. The true gospel will always draw you to Christ but counterfeits will distract you. Fake gospels result in praise to men but the true gospel will always leave you, like Mary, magnifying the Lord and rejoicing in God your Savior (Luke 1:47).

2. Does this gospel empower me to overcome sin?

Does the message I'm hearing leave me sin-conscious and condemned or cross-conscious and blameless? Does it push me to overcome sin in my own strength or does it lead me to the grace that teaches me to say no to ungodliness?

Sin is a big problem for many people. I regularly hear from people who are condemned by the sin in their lives. They desperately want to change but they feel powerless to do so.

I have learned that in the church there are two ways to deal with sin: (1) preach law or (2) reveal grace. A law-based message will stir up the flesh in a human-powered quest for a change in behavior. This approach is inherently flawed, for the purpose of the law is to inflame sin, not extinguish it (Romans 7:5). The law releases condemnation (which some mistake for conviction) and ministers death, just as it was designed to do (2 Corinthians 3:7–9).

In contrast, the gospel of grace will point you to the cross, where your sins were dealt with once and for all, and it will empower you to overcome sin by revealing your new identity in Christ.

You are not a sinner held captive to sin; you are a new creation learning to walk. Your old sin software has been nailed to the cross. You now have the same appetites and desires of Jesus. Past habits are not dealt with by laying down the law but by reckoning yourself alive to Christ. Again, the focus is on Jesus, not you. Jesus was tempted in every way yet was without sin. As you learn to rest securely in him, untroubled by the threats of old covenant agitators, you will find the grace that enables you to say no to ungodliness.

Here's the test: A counterfeit gospel will make a great show of being opposed to sin but will only drive sin underground. In contrast, the true gospel will emphasize God's greater grace that drives sin to extinction. A counterfeit gospel will make you work for forgiveness and even then leave you feeling guilty and convicted. But the true gospel reveals a forgiveness so divine it retains no memory of your sin. A counterfeit gospel promotes mask-wearing dishonesty and fills churches with phonies. But the true gospel promotes honest transparency and fills churches with testimonies of radical transformation.

3. Does this gospel release peace and joy?

Does the message I'm hearing leave me anxious and insecure or does it fill me with supernatural peace and joy? Does it emphasize my responsibility to perform *for* Christ or release a joy-filled response *to* Christ?

Not every Christian is struggling with sin. Many are just struggling. They are trying to do the right thing, trying to be pleasing to God, trying to be good Christians, but it's hard work and they are exhausted. They appear to be pillars of their churches but they are straining to hold things up. It's only a matter of time before they crack and crumble under the unholy weight of expectations.

My heart goes out to folks like this. They are sincere in their desire to serve the Lord, and they have convinced themselves it is normal for Christians to be busy little bees but it's not. We're not insects. Hebrews 4:10 says, "Anyone who enters God's rest also rests from his own work, just as God did from his." However, these folks have no time for rest. There's work to be done. They've got meetings to attend, programs to run, places to go, and people to see. They think they'll rest when they get to heaven but at the rate they're going, that's going to happen sooner rather than later.

The kingdom of God is righteousness, peace, and joy in the Holy Spirit (Romans 14:17). If the message you're listening to doesn't reveal Jesus and the gift of his righteousness, then you will never experience the peace and joy that comes with it. This test is actually about righteousness: Are you resting in his or are you trying to earn points with yours? A false gospel would have you manufacture righteousness through good works and right living but it will leave you as stressed as Martha. You'll wonder, *What has happened to my joy? Why has the laughter gone out of my marriage to Christ?*[2]

Here's the test: If you stopped doing what you are doing for Jesus, would you feel guilty? What if you sinned, stopped giving, or skipped church? Would you feel condemned? I am not encouraging you to do any of these things, but someone who knows they have been made righteous will never contend with guilt and condemnation. Conversely, someone who has bought into a false gospel will never know lasting peace. Even when they've done more than their share they will be troubled by an uneasy restlessness. *Is it enough? Does it please the Lord? Should I do more?*

Paul began every one of his letters declaring, "Grace and peace to you from God the Father." The grace of God comes wrapped in peace. When you receive grace you automatically receive peace and your soul finds rest. How do you know when you are trusting in his love and grace? You have the peace of God that guards your heart. And when you understand that the One who knew no sin became sin so that through him you might become the righteousness of God, you have joy as well.

The angel was right—the gospel brings great joy to all who receive it. It brings freedom to the captives, health to the sick, and life to the dead. The gospel is, and always has been, the power of God for your salvation.

Just as I hear from people who are struggling with sin, I also hear from others who have taken hold of this gospel of grace. Those in the second group all have unique stories but one thing they have in common is they are all full of joy. Their hearts are well-springs of laughter and they can't help but sing the praises of their God. They are living proof of Isaiah's words:

145

In that day you will say ... "Surely God is my salvation; I will trust and not be afraid. The Lord, the Lord, is my strength and my song; he has become my salvation." With joy you will draw water from the wells of salvation. (Isaiah 12:1–3)

A counterfeit gospel will turn you into a restless wanderer and leave you wondering "Have I done enough?" But the gospel of grace leaves you resting in his righteousness, secure in his love, and overflowing with peace and joy.

4. Does this gospel set me free?

Does the message I'm hearing bind me with heavy loads or does it give me a yoke that is easy and light? Does it compel me to keep the commandments or to trust in the One who fulfilled them on my behalf? Does it tie me up with cords of duty and obligation, or does it liberate me to dance under the wide skies of my Father's love and grace?

Every gospel promises freedom but the counterfeits never deliver. Those who swallow their toxic mixture of grace-plus-works become burdened again with the yoke of slavery:

Formerly, when you did not know God, you were slaves to those who by nature are not gods. But now that you know God—or rather are known by God—how is it that you are turning back to those weak and miserable principles? Do you wish to be enslaved by them all over again? (Galatians 4:8–9)

Like the Galatians, many Christians have been sold into slavery by "another gospel" (Galatians 1:6, KJV) They have been taken captive to the law that binds us and told that Christ's gift of freedom is for later, not now; his salvation is for tomorrow, not today. The message they have heard says, "If you behave yourself and stay out of trouble then maybe, one day, you will be rewarded." But when the blessings of the gospel are postponed to the distant future, all that remains for the present are the enslaving bonds of rules and traditions. When the Promised Land remains nothing but a promise, the slaves stay put in Egypt.

The true gospel declares that wherever the Spirit of the Lord is, there is liberty—not when you die, not tomorrow, but today. God's will is for you to experience the freedom of heaven here and now.

A true preacher of grace will fight fiercely for your freedom. He will smack down any teaching or doctrine that seeks to deprive you of the life and liberty that are yours in Christ, and he will draw lines in the sand so you can clearly distinguish grace from ungrace. In short, he will sound just like Paul:

> Freedom is what we have—Christ has set us free! Stand, then, as free people, and do not allow yourselves to become slaves again. (Galatians 5:1, GNB)

Here's the test. A counterfeit gospel will make you conscious of some perceived debt to Christ in order to bind you to a lifetime of indentured servitude. However, the true gospel will rip these chains off you by revealing a grace that leaves no debt and a Savior who does the heavy lifting on your behalf. A counterfeit gospel will teach you to fear authority making you a target for tyrants and manipulators. But the true gospel declares, "You were bought at a price; do not become slaves of men" (1 Corinthians 7:23). A counterfeit gospel will imprison you within the confining walls of rules and regulations, but the true gospel proclaims, "If the Son sets you free, you will be free indeed" (John 8:36).

Rate your gospel

So how did your gospel do? If you honestly answered "No" to any of these four questions, then you have been sold a toxic gospel. Discard it before it kills you! But don't shoot the messengers. As someone who used to preach a counterfeit gospel I have nothing but grace for those who still do. Most of them love the Lord just as much as you or I. So love them but don't listen to them—not if they're leading you away from grace.

If you answered "Yes" to all four questions then rejoice, for you are living on pure, undiluted grace. You have gotten hold of the authentic gospel and you will go far.

The best news you ever heard

Grace and ungrace don't mix. How do you recognize the authentic gospel? It's 100 percent good news. There's no bad news in the good news. There's no price tag on the gift, no hooks in his love, and no shadows in the light. The gospel proclaims that in union with Christ you are loved, forgiven, saved, accepted, holy, righteous, dead to sin, new, and royal. The gospel is good news from start to finish.

In this book we have looked at ten facets of the gospel of grace. Here they are in summary form:

1. The gospel is not a solicitation to impress God with your love; it is the passionate declaration of your Father's undying love for you.
2. The gospel is not an appeal to engage in soul-searching and fault-finding; it is the emphatic declaration that you have been completely and eternally forgiven through the blood of the Lamb.
3. The gospel is not merely a promise of a ticket to heaven; it is the power of God to bless you with his saving and abundant life here and now.
4. The gospel is not an advertising brochure for the treasures of the kingdom; it is the thrilling revelation that the Lover of your soul desires to share his life in wedded union with you forever.
5. The gospel is not an invitation to accept Jesus; it is the stunning announcement that he accepts you.
6. The gospel is not a sign-up sheet for sanctification classes; it is the definitive announcement that in Christ you are holy indeed.
7. The gospel is not a list of things you must do to inherit eternal life; it is the blessed announcement that

the righteousness you need to enter the kingdom of heaven comes to us as a free gift through faith.

8. The gospel is not a reform program for bad people; it is the liberating declaration of new life for those who have died.

9. The gospel is not a half-baked hope that you can extend your old, broken life indefinitely; it is the joyful announcement that in Christ the old has gone and the new has come.

10. The gospel is not a vague notion that you get to rule and reign after you die; it is the royal announcement that the reign of the King is within the reach of faith. The kingdom of God is at hand.

Two thousand years ago Grace personified proclaimed the gospel to some folks in Nazareth. As we come to the end of this book, let us imagine ourselves sitting in the synagogue listening to Jesus speak these words:

> The Spirit of the Lord is on me, because he has anointed me to preach good news to the poor. He has sent me to proclaim freedom for the prisoners and recovery of sight for the blind, to release the oppressed, to proclaim the year of the Lord's favor ... Today this scripture is fulfilled in your hearing. (Luke 4:18–19, 21)

The good news is the best news you ever heard. The good news declares that no matter who you are or where you have come from, today is the day of your salvation, and this is the year of the Lord's favor.

The adventure of living loved has just begun!

If you enjoyed reading *The Gospel in Ten Words*, you can find Paul's latest writings at www.escapetoreality.org

NOTES

Out of the Jungle
1. Hiroo Onoda, *No Surrender: My Thirty-Year War*, Kodansha, 1974.
2. See Romans 8:31–32 and Isaiah 54:8–10. See also 1 Timothy 1:11 in Rotherham's Emphasized Bible which describes the "glorious gospel of the blessed God" as the "glad-message of the glory of the happy God."
3. "Sermon No.2207," The Spurgeon Archive, website: www.spurgeon.org/sermons/2207.htm
4. Sources for these gospels are as follows: Paul (1 Corinthians 2:2), Peter (Acts 2:36), John (John 1:17), and Jesus (John 14:6).
5. "Jesus Loves Me," Wikipedia, website: en.wikipedia.org/wiki/Jesus_Loves_-Me. While looking for an official source for this popular Sunday school song, I discovered the "Senior Version" penned by an anonymous author. Possibly inspired by Isaiah 46:4, it's the gospel for seniors. The opening verse is as follows: "Jesus loves me, this I know / Though my hair is white as snow / Though my sight is growing dim / Still he bids me trust in him."
6. "The gospel in one word, two words ..." EscapeToReality.org, 22 March 2011, website: wp.me/pNzdT-JS
7. "Former WWII soldier visits Philippine hideout," CNN.com, 26 May 1996, website: edition.cnn.com/WORLD/9605/26/philippines.straggler/

Chapter 1: Loved
1. See Isaiah 54:8 and Psalms 30:5.
2. Here's a tip for preachers: They say people need to hear truth several times before they finally get it. When it comes to the love of God, err on the side of over-doing it. Follow the example of the writer of Psalm 136 who declared the enduring love or loving-kindness (*hesed*) of God no less than 26 times. The love of God is a drum worth banging loudly and often. Since his unending love surpasses knowledge (Ephesians 3:19), there is no danger of exaggeration.
3. C.S. Lewis, *The Silver Chair*, Lions, 1953/1980, p.145.
4. See Jeremiah 31:3, Romans 8:38–39, and 1 Corinthians 13:7–8.
5. See Romans 5:5, 15:30, Colossians 1:8, 2 Timothy 1:7.

Chapter 2: Forgiven
1. In Luke 24:47 Jesus describes forgiveness as a noun (*aphesis* in Greek) starting a pattern followed by the New Testament epistle writers. Prior to the cross, God's forgiveness is almost always described as a verb (*aphiemi*). After the cross it is almost always a noun.
2. Long before Jesus was born, the two great prophets Isaiah and Jeremiah looked forward to a time when God would blot out our transgressions and remember our sins no more (see Isaiah 43:25, 44:22 and Jeremiah 31:33–34). In Hebrews chapters 8 to 10 (and particularly 8:10–12 and 10:16–17) we learn that these prophecies were fulfilled at the cross. For a sample of radical grace-based psalms, check out Psalms 23, 36, 85, 103, 117, 121, and 145.
3. To the religious mind, grace sounds like blasphemy. How ironic considering that there is nothing more blasphemous or slanderous than self-righteously

refusing to believe the Holy Spirit's testimony regarding the grace of God revealed through Jesus Christ (Mark 3:29).

4. G3670 (*homologeo*), Thayer's Greek Lexicon, website: concordances.org/-greek/3670.htm

5. Jesus said many will try to enter the narrow door of salvation and will not be able to (Luke 13:23-24). This is not because God is selective with us, but we are selective with him. Grace is for everyone but not everyone is for grace.

6. Paul referred to the law as the "ministry that brought death" (2 Corinthians 3:7). But note that it's not the law that kills people, it's sin. "Once I was alive apart from law; but when the commandment came, sin sprang to life and I died" (Romans 7:9). The law activates the sin that was there all along.

7. In the first chapter of his letter, John says "we" a lot—*we* need to be purified from sin, *we* need to confess our sins, etc.—prompting some to think he is referring to "we Christians." If this is the case, then John's theology is out of step with the other epistle writers. Those who already have fellowship with Christ and his body (1 Corinthians 1:9) do not need to be invited into that fellowship (1 John 1:3). Neither do those who have already heard and believed the message (Romans 10:17) need to hear the message that John has heard (1 John 1:5). Christians have heard the truth and walk in the light (John 8:12, 2 John 1:4), but those whom John addresses do not live by the truth and walk in darkness (1 John 1:6). Since there is nothing wrong with John's theology, we can only conclude that, in chapter 1, he is not addressing Christians. Consider: Christians have been purified from all sin (Hebrews 10:1-14), but those John writes to need to be purified from all sin (1 John 1:9). Christians agree with God (Romans 10:9-13), but those John addresses are calling God a liar (1 John 1:10). God's word lives in Christians (1 Thessalonians 2:13) but it does not live in them (1 John 1:10). Don't build a theology of confession on one little word. John uses the word "we" in a pastoral sense of identifying with his unsaved listeners. *We* all have sinned and fall short and *we* all need to come to Jesus but some of us already have. John writes for the whole world. Chapter 1 is mainly directed to those who don't know Jesus ("*You* need to have fellowship with him") while chapter 2 is directed to those who do ("My dear children …"). Sometimes the chapter divisions do make sense.

8. Brennan Manning, *The Ragamuffin Gospel*, Multnomah, 1990/2000, pp.123-129. This is just one of many good stories in Manning's book.

9. Too strong do you think? Yet Jesus uses similar words when dealing with the mask-wearing Maxes of Laodicea (Revelation 3:16).

10. See Romans 4:8 and 2 Corinthians 5:18-19.

11. This classic youth group song is based on Ephesians 1:7.

Chapter 3: Saved

1. See Romans 3:23, 6:23.

2. A friend asked me to explain how salvation can be free in light of the high cost of discipleship. Jesus said, "Any of you who does not give up everything he has cannot be my disciple" (Luke 14:33). He also said, "Freely you have received" (Matthew 10:8). So which is it? Is salvation free or does it cost us everything? It's both. The gift is free but you can only receive it with empty

hands. The cost is you have to let go of your old life in order to receive his new life. You can't have a bet each way. If you would follow the Savior you must forsake all other saviors including yourself.

3. Paul's warning about other gospels and those who preach them is found in Galatians 1:6–9. "If anyone preaches to you a gospel that is different from the one you accepted, may he be condemned to hell!" (GNB). Similar warnings were made by Jesus (Matthew 7:15–23), Peter (2 Peter 2:1–3), John (1 John 4:1–3) and Jude (Jude 1:4).

4. See Acts 2:21, 4:12, 17:30, 1 Timothy 2:4 and 1 John 3:23. Jesus preached a consistent message of salvation through faith before and after the cross. Before the cross it was, "Whoever believes in me may have eternal life" (John 3:15); after the cross it was "Whoever believes will be saved" (see Mark 16:16).

5. The wonderfully affirming "whosoever calls" message was proclaimed by Peter (Acts 2:21), Paul (Romans 10:13), and no doubt the other apostles as well. They wanted believers to have a secure assurance of their salvation. Incidentally, in case you were wondering why a chapter entitled "Saved" came third and not first in a book on the gospel, the answer has to do with John the Baptist's dad. When Zacharias got his speech back, he prophesied that his son would "give his people the knowledge of salvation *through the forgiveness of their sins*" (Luke 1:77). Salvation comes through forgiveness. Because you are forgiven, you can be saved. Because your sins have been removed, you can receive the gift of his righteousness.

6. A friend of mine likes to tell new believers, "If you fall in the kingdom, you fall *in* the kingdom."

7. The success of the lifeboat gospel may also explain why the church is full of women and children.

8. G4982 (*sozo*), Strong's Exhaustive Concordance, website: concordances.org/-greek/4982.htm

9. Not everyone I have prayed for has been healed. Since healing is one part of the salvation package, the temptation is to think, "If God couldn't heal this person, perhaps he can't save me." This is a lie from the pit of hell that will fill you with doubt and render you impassive with unbelief. Any healing should be celebrated as a miracle. It is proof that God wants to heal, that he does heal, and he does it through us. "Well, what about those that don't get healed? What does that show us?" It tells me that we're still learning. Why would Paul exhort the Philippians to "go for it all the more in my absence" if they only ever experienced success? Like us they needed encouraging. "Keep going. Don't give up because you've had a few setbacks. A sick and dying world is waiting for the experienced and mature sons of God to be revealed." Paul also said that God is able to do "immeasurably more than all we ask or imagine, according to his power that is at work within us" (Ephesians 3:20). God's power works *within us*. There is something about *us* that releases or restrains the power of God. We're still learning but Jesus isn't. Every single person who came to him for healing was healed. Similarly, every single person who comes to him for salvation is saved (see Hebrews 7:24–25). No exceptions.

10. See Matthew 9:22 and Mark 5:34 in the KJV.

Chapter 4: Union

1. Many Christians are worried that they are going to be cut off on account of sin, bitterness, or barrenness. The only way that could happen, given the connate nature of our union with Christ, is if Jesus decides to be unfaithful to himself. In other words, it's not going to happen. "If we are faithless, he will remain faithful, for he cannot disown himself" (2 Timothy 2:13). What happens to unfruitful branches? Jesus said the branches that don't bear fruit are "lifted up" (John 15:2). They are not cut off. That is a bad translation that doesn't fit the context. Jesus used the Greek word *airo* which can mean taken or lifted up (see Matthew 16:24 for such an interpretation). Unfruitful branches are lifted out of the dirt and redressed so the sun can nourish them. Sticking with that metaphor, the reason some Christians are barren is they are face down in the dirt and not basking in the light and love of the Son. Fruit follows intimacy.
2. See Romans 8:9, Colossians 2:9, and John 14:20.
3. These lyrics of longing come from Song of Songs 3:1–2, 5:6 and Psalms 42:1.
4. Just as Isaac was born in the power of the Spirit (Galatians 4:29), you were born into your new life by the Holy Spirit. "It is the Spirit who gives life [*He is the Life-giver*]" (John 6:63, AMP). The Holy Spirit is both the means by which you first entered into union and the sign that you are now in union. "We are sure that we live in union with God and that he lives in union with us, because he has given us his Spirit" (1 John 4:13, GNB).
5. G4854 (*sumphutos*), Thayer's and Smith's Bible Dictionary, website: www.biblestudytools.com/lexicons/greek/kjv/sumphutos.html. Like Dr. Strong, these lexicographers interpret the word as meaning *connate* which comes from the Latin word conatus, from *con*- "together" and *nasci* "be born." The Oxford English Dictionary defines *connate* as "(of parts) united so as to form a single part." Website: oxforddictionaries.com/definition/connate.
6. Paul addressed the Philippian Christians as the "saints in Christ Jesus" (Philippians 1:1) and then exhorted those saints to greet all the other "saints in Christ Jesus" (Philippians 4:21). Just as there are no saints outside of Christ Jesus, there are no sinners in Christ Jesus. If you are in him, you are a saint.
7. See Isaiah 24:16 and Jeremiah 23:5, 33:15.
8. In scripture, the desire for union is often expressed as a calling to fellowship or *koinonia* (see, for example, 1 Corinthians 1:9 and 1 John 1:2–3). *Koinonia* literally means participating in the life of God that is in Christ Jesus. It is another word for the spiritual union all believers have in common with Christ.

Chapter 5: Accepted

1. Jesus' acceptance of frail Peter is recorded in Luke 22:31–34. Jesus' acceptance of Judas as "friend" is recorded in Matthew 26:50.
2. Dr. Seuss, *Oh, the Places You'll Go!*, HarperCollins, 1957/1990.
3. Source unknown. To the best of my knowledge, announcements similar to this one were first heard in mid-western Catholic and Lutheran churches in the early 2000s.

Chapter 6: Holy

1. Isaiah and John both had visions of heaven. Isaiah heard six-winged seraphs singing "Holy, holy, holy is the Lord Almighty; the whole earth is full of his glory" (Isaiah 6:3). John saw four living creatures who never stop saying, "Holy, holy, holy is the Lord God Almighty, who was, and is, and is to come" (Revelation 4:8).
2. For regulations forbidding trimmed beards see Leviticus 19:17; for tattoos see Leviticus 19:28; for bacon see Leviticus 11:7. Lepers who wanted to be holy had it particularly tough as they were deemed untouchable and had to go around in mourning clothes shouting "Unclean! Unclean!" (Leviticus 13:45).
3. G5046 (*teleios*), Strong's Exhaustive Concordance, website: concordances.org/greek/5046.htm
4. This is a reference to Jesus' ministry as our high priest. "Although he was a son, he learned obedience from what he suffered and, once made perfect, he became the source of eternal salvation for all who obey him and was designated by God to be high priest in the order of Melchizedek." (Hebrews 5:8-10). As God's Son, Jesus was sinless and perfect. But he could not represent us and free us from captivity until he had identified with our death. "Since the children have flesh and blood, he too shared in their humanity so that by his death he might destroy him who holds the power of death – that is, the devil – and free those who all their lives were held in slavery by their fear of death" (Hebrews 2:14-15). God demands eternal perfection. Either you must be perfect or you must be represented by one who is. A high priest such as Jesus meets our need – One who is holy, blameless, pure, and exalted above the heavens (Hebrews 7:26).
5. Most gym instructors will tell you that your holiness requires an act of your will combined with the daily sacrifice of your body. But Hebrews 10:10 says, "By that will" meaning the will of God, "we have been made holy through the sacrifice of the body of Jesus Christ once for all." It's a simple equation: His will plus his sacrifice equals our holiness, once for all.
6. To paraphrase Psalm 34:10, "The young (immature) lions may grow weak and hungry (become needy), but those who trust the Lord lack no good thing (are whole, their needs amply supplied)." To put it another way, those who look to the flesh to meet their needs will remain incomplete, but in him you are complete – wholly whole and lacking nothing.
7. Note that the NIV translation of 1 Peter 2:5 says you "are being built... to be a holy priesthood" which sounds as though you are not presently holy. However, Young's Literal Translation of that passage conveys the more accurate sense that you are being built up *as* a holy priesthood. The NIV translators would agree with this interpretation. Four verses later they note that you are, right now, "a chosen people, a royal priesthood, a holy nation" (1 Peter 2:9).

Chapter 7: Righteous

1. See Revelation 3:1-6. How do we soil our clothes? By trying to make ourselves righteous. "Our righteous acts are like filthy rags" (Isaiah 64:6). What is appropriate attire in God's eyes? Being clothed with Christ and the robe of *his* righteousness (Isaiah 61:10). These two kinds of righteousness – ours and

his—are mutually exclusive. But don't make Luther's mistake of thinking that "Christians are snow-covered dung." You are not righteous on the outside and rotten on the inside. In union with the Lord you are as righteous as he is (see 2 Corinthians 5:21).

2. G5526 (*chortazó*), Strong's Exhaustive Concordance, website: concordances.org/greek/5526.htm

3. Surely you don't need a scripture to back this up but if you do, here are fourteen: Acts 13:39, Romans 1:17, 3:22, 28, 4:5, 24, 5:1, 9:30, 10:6, Galatians 2:16, 3:8,24, Phlippians 3:9, Hebrews 11:7.

4. At least two accusers are identified in the Bible. One is the law, a.k.a. Moses (John 5:45), and the other is the devil (Revelation 12:10). The Holy Spirit accuses no one of sin, not even sinners. Jesus said the Holy Spirit would convict the world "in regard to sin *because men do not believe in me*" (John 16:9). The issue is not wrongdoing but unbelief. (Wrongdoing follows wrong believing.) To blaspheme or slander or speak falsely of the Holy Spirit is to refuse to allow him to convince you that Jesus is the once and final solution for sin.

5. See Ezekiel 3:20, 18:24–26, 33:13. In the Old Testament, even your best righteousness wasn't good enough. Elihu asked Job whether he seriously thought that his righteousness was better than God's righteousness (see Job 35:2). In case Job had any doubts, Elihu pointed out that just as God is unaffected by our wickedness, so is he also unimpressed by our righteousness (Job 35:8). It was a lesson lost on the Israelites. God flat out told them, "I will expose your righteousness and your works, and they will not benefit you" (Isaiah 57:12). Jesus said something similar: "Unless your righteousness surpasses that of the Pharisees and the teachers of the law, you will certainly not enter the kingdom of heaven" (Matthew 5:20). The point? Our righteousness doesn't pass muster. We need the righteousness he freely provides.

Chapter 8: Died

1. See Colossians 2:20, Romans 6:8, and 2 Corinthians 5:14.

2. Didn't Paul say he died daily? He did (see 1 Corinthians 15:31–32), but he was referring to the dangers and hardships he faced in preaching the gospel. "I fought wild beasts in Ephesus!" He was not preaching a works-based theology of dying to self. Paul understood that you don't crucify the new man. We don't die to self, we died to the law (Romans 7:4, Galatians 2:19)—including the law that says we must die to self.

3. Watchman Nee, *The Normal Christian Life*, Tyndale House, 1977, p.52. Nee asks, "Must we ask God to crucify us? Never! When Christ was crucified we were crucified; and his crucifixion is past therefore ours cannot be future" (pp.44–45).

4. The Greek verb for sin is *hamartano⁻* (G264 in the Strong's numbering system). However, Paul uses the noun *hamartia* (G266) in Romans 5:12, 6:12, 14, 17, 20 and 7:11, 14, 20 and about 40 other places in Romans.

5. If this is not clear to you, read Galatians 2:16–21 in the Message Bible and the lights should go on.

Chapter 9: New

1. G2537 (*kainos*), Thayer's Greek Lexicon, website: concordances.-org/greek/2537.htm

2. Sources for the poem "Who am I?": I am a saint (Ephesians 1:1, Philippians 1:1 Jude 1:3), a trophy of Christ's victory (2 Corinthians 2:14, AMP); born of imperishable seed (1 Peter 1:23), a new creation (2 Corinthians 5:17); complete in Christ (Colossians 2:10, KJV) and perfect forever (Hebrews 10:14); a child of God (1 John 3:1), the apple of my Father's eye (Psalms 17:8); one with the Lord (1 Corinthians 6:17) and the temple of the Holy Spirit (1 Corinthians 6:19); eternally redeemed (Hebrews 7:25, 9:12) and completely forgiven (Colossians 2:13); seated with Christ in heavenly places (Ephesians 2:6); righteous (2 Corinthians 5:21), holy and blameless (Ephesians 1:4); hidden in Christ (Colossians 3:3) and eternally secure (Hebrews 6:19); my beloved's and he is mine (Song of Songs 6:3); the head and not the tail (Deuteronomy 28:13); blessed with every spiritual blessing (Ephesians 1:3), a joint heir with Christ (Romans 8:17); a competent minister of the new covenant (2 Corinthians 3:6); bona fide and qualified (Colossians 1:12), chosen (John 15:19, Colossians 3:12, 1 Peter 2:9) and anointed (1 John 2:27); his royal ambassador (2 Corinthians 5:20), a missionary to the world (Matthew 28:19); as bold as a lion (Proverb 28:1) and more than a conqueror (Romans 8:37); the salt (Matthew 5:13) and light of the world (Matthew 5:14); the sweet smell of Jesus to those who are perishing (2 Corinthians 2:15); a tree planted by the water (Psalms 1:3, Jeremiah 17:8), and a fruitful branch (John 15:8); king o' the world (Revelation 1:6, 1 John 5:4) because His victory is mine (1 Corinthians 15:57); the disciple whom Jesus loves (Romans 5:5, Ephesians 1:6) and by the grace of God I am what I am (1 Corinthians 15:10).

3. Jesus even chose a thief to be one of his disciples (see John 12:4-6).

4. See 1 John 2:1 and Hebrews 5:2

5. See 1 Peter 1:13, 1 John 1:7, 2:6.

6. See Ephesians 1:15-23, Philemon 1:6.

Chapter 10: Royal

1. At the time of Christ there was a two-tier priest system; an A-team consisting of the scribes and Pharisees and a B-team consisting of regular Levites. That two-tier system persists today in the clergy-laity distinction found within some institutional churches. However, in the New Testament church, it is not apparent that there was any such distinction. Every Christian is, by definition, a royal priest serving under Jesus our high priest (see 1 Peter 2:9, 2 Corinthians 3:6).

2. H7287 (*râdâh*), Strong's Exhaustive Concordance, website: concordances.org/hebrew/7287.htm

3. The first time God ever said the word "king" was in this promise made to Abraham (see Genesis 17:6), a promise he repeated to both Sarah (Genesis 17:16) and Jacob (Genesis 35:11).

4. See Matthew 10:1, 8, 12:28, Mark 16:17-20, Luke 10:19, and John 14:12.

5. A bad report or the sight of a crippling disease can inflame natural unbelief. At such times we have to "be zealous and exert ourselves and strive diligently

to enter that rest [*of God, to know and experience it for ourselves*]" (Hebrews 4:11, AMP).

6.   Job's story is found in Job 1:13-15, 20 and 2:8. David's story is found in 1 Samuel 30:1-19.

The Test of Your Gospel

1.   I once heard a well-known preacher say that "80 to 90 percent of Christians are unacquainted with the gospel of grace." Another notable teacher put that mark at closer to 95 percent. These are astonishing figures, yet I think they are sadly accurate.

2.   See Galatians 4:15, Job 8:21, and Psalms 126:2.

SCRIPTURE INDEX

FAQs

ACKNOWLEDGEMENTS

I have been the beneficiary of God's grace my entire life. Through family, friends, and sometimes complete strangers, I have long enjoyed the unmerited favor of my heavenly Father. But if I was to single out my earliest exposure to the gospel of grace, it would be a VHS taped message I first saw in 1996. The preacher on the tape was a fiery South African who had such a way with words he could've been a poet. Not long after that I met Rob Rufus in person and we have been friends ever since. Thanks, Rob, for being as dogged and passionate as the Apostle Paul in your preaching of the gospel of grace.

Every chapter in this book was read by at least three other people prior to publication. The multinational group of reviewers involved in this process included: Steve Barker, Michael Beil, Chris Blackeby, Steve Hackman, Tammy Hackman, Febe Kuey, Cornel Marais, Andre van der Merwe, Brandon Petrowski, Ryan Rhoades, Ryan Rufus, Gaye Stradwick, Peter Wilson, and Gerry Zitzmann. I greatly appreciate the feedback and encouragement provided by my brothers and sisters in grace. Of course, any errors that remain in the book are my fault, not theirs. I am also grateful to Adrienne Morris who proofread the whole manuscript.

I want to thank the many hundreds of people who have written to me privately and via discussion threads on my blog to encourage, criticize, debate, and otherwise push me towards a deeper understanding of God's love and grace. I would also like to thank those of you who had nothing to say but who encouraged me nonetheless by clicking the "Share" buttons under my posts. It never ceases to amaze me that with the click of a button one can send an encouraging word of grace all around the world.

My biggest thanks goes to my wife Camilla who provided me with a quiet environment in which to write. She was also the first to read every word written and she painstakingly checked the accuracy of all 454 scriptures references in this book. Everyone blessed by my writings owes a debt of gratitude to Camilla for she is my sounding board. She is the first to hear every revelation I get. If what I say makes her smile, you hear it; if it doesn't, you don't. Camilla is my daily reminder of God's grace and a shining light to all who know her.

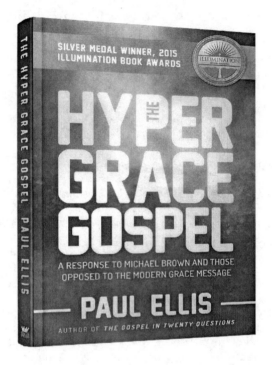

**2015 Christian Small Publisher Book of the Year
(Christian Living category)**

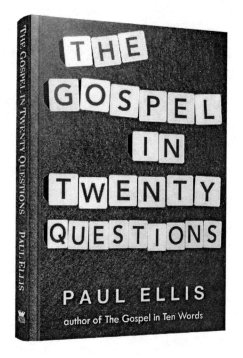

"One of the best books I have ever read..." — ED ELLIOTT, Word of Life
World Outreach

"Another home run!" — PAUL C. MATA, Word for All Nations, Philippines

"Bursting with divine goodness!" — CORNEL MARAIS, Charisma Ministries

AVAILABLE NOW!

www.20qns.com

CPSIA information can be obtained
at www.ICGtesting.com
Printed in the USA
FSOW02n0327311017
40410FS